CRACKING OPEN

Daphne
Publications

Also by Bud Harris, Ph.D.

Sacred Selfishness: A Guide to Living a Life of Substance

The Father Quest: Rediscovering an Elemental Force

Resurrecting the Unicorn: Masculinity in the 21st Century

The Fire and the Rose: The Wedding of Spirituality and Sexuality

Knowing the Questions Living the Answers: A Jungian Guide Through the Paradoxes of Peace, Conflict and Love that Mark a Lifetime

Coauthored with Massimilla Harris, Ph.D.:

Like Gold Through Fire: Understanding the Transforming Power of Suffering

The Art of Love: The Craft of Relationships: A Practical Guide for Creating the Loving Relationships We Want

Into the Heart of the Feminine: An Archetypal Journey to Renew Strength, Love, and Creativity

CRACKING OPEN

A Memoir of Struggling, Passages, and Transformations

BUD HARRIS, PH.D.

DAPHNE PUBLICATIONS • ASHEVILLE, NORTH CAROLINA

Contents

This element in man as keeper of the vision of life
in all its fullness and triumphant wholeness
is ultimately concerned with a journey made not on foot
nor donkey, camel, horse or ox-wagon, ship or aeroplane,
but a journey from one state of being to another,
a journey of becoming.

– LAURENS VAN DER POST

Introduction: 2015

The great principle of transformation begins through the things that are lowest.
Things…that hide from the light of day and from man's enlightened thinking
hold also the secret of life that renews itself again and again.
In the past when a transformation of this kind was sought,
the mystery religions prescribed a ritual of initiation.

— C. G. JUNG

It has taken me a long time to fully realize that destruction is an opening to transformation, even though I knew it in my head. Themes of destruction and creation underlie our lives. If I follow the lines of thinking in my religion, creation is for the sake of redemption, but between these two poles are many moments of destruction. I was surprised when a colleague, Jungian analyst and author Charlotte Mathes, saw this in my life. In her gracious endorsement of my book *The Fire and the Rose,* she said about me, "He generously shares how his deepest early wound began a struggle to redefine perceptions of God and to make tough choices about money, vocation, family and authentic relationship to Self and community." I have done a lot of inner work, but strange enough, even though I was well aware of how difficult my life was, I had never thought of myself as seriously wounded. Yet I clearly was. I have never thought of myself as having had a breakdown either, though, Lord knows, other people must have thought so. Perhaps I had read too many books growing up and become too romantic in how I looked at life. I know very well that I have had periods of loss and despair, even long ones.

I have also had at least four periods of what I refer to as "periods of ashes." During these times I compare my experiences with the legend of the phoenix and the real-world growth process of crabs, called molt-ing. In Greek mythology, the phoenix is a bird that transforms itself by setting fire to its own nest, letting itself be consumed by the flames until it emerges from the fire, reborn as a new creature. The crab grows while its shell does not. At a certain point, it must molt, shedding its shell, or be killed by its own growth. At that point, it secretes a fluid that loosens the shell until the crab can carefully squeeze its way out of the old shell. Then without a shell for protection, it must hide itself away in the nooks and crannies on the ocean floor until it grows a new shell. Three times in my adult life, I have walked away from all that I had accomplished. I burned my own nest, or more likely squeezed out of the old shell that was choking my whole being to death. I didn't disdain the things I walked away from. Even as I look back on my life today, I am still proud of my accomplishments. I honor them and the learning and struggle that I endured to attain them. My struggles as well as my accomplishments became part of the foundation of my future. I also suffered in the process because it is my nature to be fully engaged in what I do, and when I came to the place where transformation was necessary for my survival and growth, I didn't want to disengage. Sometimes I hid, hoping the need would go away. But it didn't. Life was calling at some level, and I knew that if I didn't answer, part of me, or maybe all of me, would perish.

The phoenix is consumed by a fire of its own making, and the crab, totally vulnerable, must shrink into hiding in the safety of darkness. These are not appealing options. Transformation is not easy and there is no reason to think it should be. Popular culture urges us to seek happiness, and if we want to grow further, the popular perspective teaches that our growth should be leading us toward a blissful path—peace, balance, compassion, and enlightenment. But this is a partial story. Centuries ago, the Greek playwright Aeschylus elegantly informed us that wisdom is wrung from our tears, drop by drop. Transformations are never easy and are seldom blissful. They are filled with doubt, angst, fear, courage, love, and loneliness. And yet they unite us with one another, with life, and with the Divine. The archetypal pattern of transformation—life, death, and rebirth—that is central in our myths and great religions tells us that when we are in the dark, we must strive with all of our hearts for new light. We must learn to understand that when we think there is only an end, we must struggle for a new beginning. Dark and light, endings and beginnings—these are cyclical stages in transformation that we must either embrace or hide from. However, in hiding, we turn our back to the call of our life. I consider anything that diminishes life as evil, but, oh how often, I have longed to hide.

This reminds me of the Old Testament story of Jacob, who had set out on a journey. When night came and he had stopped to rest, he had a dream. In the dream, he saw a stairway that reached from the ground up to heaven. Angels were going up and down the stairway. I like to imagine that this dream came to tell him that the Divine plan is not for us to stay at the same stage in life. Some angels were going up and some were coming down, and this is the pattern we should follow. We must strive to reach the top—to, like the phoenix, participate fully in our transformation. Once one cycle is complete, we must then come down, either because our circumstances cause us to fall or because we have outgrown the shell of our current life. Then, as we begin to ascend once again from the bottom to the top, the cycle continues. This is an archetypal pattern that we must fully engage in, if we are to be fully alive.

If we can grasp this creative pattern of life that wants to be lived through us, and include the development of self-knowledge and consciousness in the rhythm of our lives, then we can discover a central element in ourselves, called the Self, and the spark of the Divine within us. To enable this Self to become a center in our experience and for the Self to create and hold a vision for our lives, we must struggle to this awareness and relationship *personally* through developing self-knowledge. The struggle refines us, whereas simply accepting the idea of the Self intellectually, or naively accepting some notions of the Divine from some collective dogma or institution, rarely has the same effect.

Discovering that the Self is our true center, and that it has been working in our lives all along, connects us to the creative heart of life. Symbols of the Self abound, frequently in the form of mandalas and in divine figures in mythology. The presence of the Self is often represented by gold, a symbol of our highest value. Our ability to give full expression to our true Self leads us into a sense of wholeness and peace that comes from feeling at home in life, full as it is with challenges and disasters. This journey of discovery and fulfillment is one of becoming, a journey from one state of existence to another. It is a journey into being that results from coming home to ourselves and departing again and again, like the angels on Jacob's ladder.

✳ ✳ ✳

As you read this book, you will discover that my formal journaling stops at a certain point, and my Muse shifts me into writing the story of a major turning point in my adult life in 1972. You can, perhaps, imagine my surprise when the context of the story I was telling shifted yet again, and I found myself back in my admission interviews with Dr. John Mattern in 1985 at the C. G. Jung Institute in Zurich, Switzerland, telling him my story. I was surprised, as you may be, when his "voice" showed up in the narrative. But I wrote as the story unfolded within me and, as a result, went from journaling about my current thoughts and experiences to writing a story, with scenes that shift, almost like they do in dreams. Of course, I have added chapter titles, subtitles, and quotation marks. I am a writer and I can't resist giving form to my writing.

When I returned to my journal entries to craft them into a memoir, it became clear to me that I had gained still newer reflections and insights into my spiritual and personal growth. The work that I intended to complete in 1994 has been ongoing. Even today, I am a person who is "becoming," not yet fully arrived. As a writer, I felt it was natural to add an epilogue in 2015, which includes observations and insights from my professional training that helped give me clarity and a better grasp on my life. In crafting the epilogue, I significantly enhanced my self-understanding and provided mileposts for my inner development. I hope the account of this journey is as helpful for you as it has been for me.

The people in this book are all real people who affected my life in powerful ways. What I share with you are my perceptions and remembrances—many from childhood—and how they touched my life. As I recount incidents, I am recalling the truth of my experiences and my imagination. I am not trying to give a true kind of character analysis or an in-depth assessment, so please do not evaluate any one of the people in my story based on my few words. Their lives were much more complex than the short vignettes that I share.

❊ ❊ ❊

As I look back on my life, I believe that my destiny was to become a Jungian analyst. The only problem was that it took me four and a half decades to figure that out. During that time, destiny was chipping away at me, sculpting me like Michelangelo bringing a figure out of stone. It took me all of that time to realize that the peace I sought came only after accepting that life is one crisis after another, and that every crisis is also either an opportunity to gain more personal consciousness, a deeper understanding of what it means to be human, and be transformed or an opportunity to shrink from transformation and be diminished by life.

Psychology was my second career, which began when I was thirty-five years old. Before that, I was a businessman, and as you might imagine, such a dramatic career change was the result of a transforming crisis in my life. I experienced another such crisis when I was forty-six. All in all, I experienced three of these crises before I was fifty. I like to call these times "periods of ashes" because the despair I experienced reminds me of the tradition of mourning that the Bible describes, in which mourners dressed in sackcloth sit in ashes, weeping, wailing, and gnashing their teeth. This is a far more active and realistic depiction of suffering than is suggested by our modern notion of "clinical depression," which tends to debilitate rather than transform. The passion of real despair can provide the transformational fire needed for the rise of a phoenix from our depth. In my experience, a phoenix rarely rises from our medical or behaviorally based psychological treatments of depression.

In fact, a frustration with psychological approaches—the feeling that somehow modern psychology had missed the boat—cropped up during my third period of ashes, when I realized that despite my previous therapy and professional training, I was back in the ashes. This happened in 1983, and driven by inner angst, I began to search for a deeper understanding of myself and to broaden my knowledge of human nature and development. Shortly after that, I moved to Zurich, devoting myself to an inner journey and to becoming a Jungian analyst. I completed my training there in 1989.

In the summer of 1994, I embarked on another period of transformation. This one wasn't a crisis or a period of ashes. It concluded with a dream that affirmed my decision to share the contents of my journals. I had spent an evening rereading my midsummer journal entries and a story they had given birth to. I was debating with myself whether to share these reflections and their ensuing story with others. In other words, I was debating whether I should make them public. These reflections were personal and represented experiences that both shaped and became expressions of my soul. I felt extremely shy about exposing them to the eyes and voices of others, especially those close to me who might misunderstand or criticize them. But, as you can see, I have decided to share my work, and I made that decision before going to sleep that night. In fact, I recall wondering how my unconscious would respond to my decision.

Shortly after midnight, I awoke from a deeply experienced dream that was filled with symbols of inner tranquility, wisdom, and wholeness. As I sat in the dark, I saw the lake in front of the house where I grew up. There was no wind, and the surface of the lake was still. The image was beautiful, and in a strange way, it seemed to span almost my entire life. At the center of the lake—where the water was deepest and where, beneath its surface, springs fed its depth—was an ancient rowboat. Strong and heavy, the boat was made of a dark wood that had weathered many storms. Standing in the boat, as if rooted in it, was an immense monk. His cowl was pushed back, exposing silver hair above serene blue eyes. His countenance expressed at once the experience of age, great vitality, and peace. He stood calmly fishing in the deep water.

Physically, the monk resembled me, though my eyes are not blue, and his other facial features were not clear. But certainly he is a part of

16

me, perhaps an image from my own depths, endorsing the closure of my writing project and the decision to share it. Thus ended my internal debate. However, because my work is so personal, it has taken me twenty years to carry out the decision.

❊ ❊ ❊

I concluded years ago that the traumas of my childhood and early adulthood directed my life toward a particular trajectory and the discovery of my vocation. After spending many years during my professional training exploring my early life, I am still able to find riches and lost worlds in my past. At times, I feel like a seasoned archaeologist, working for decades on a single site that is filled with discoveries. On occasion, at the end of a painstaking excavation, just when I think the work is surely finished, I find a clue to some yet unknown culture, another layer down.

As involved as my early childhood and adult experiences are, one thing is clear: They produced a desperate amount of suffering that, over time, led me in surprising directions. These directions opened for me because, no matter what, I worked like "holy hell" on my excavations, on understanding myself and my life until my suffering became the guiding star that led my spirit into the land of new birth.

I know that I cannot repeat a single moment of my past. As a practicing Jungian analyst, I also know that self-understanding lies deep within the stories of my origins. I see self-knowledge as the key to my health and my ability to renew, or rather to help myself be re-created at critical junctures in my life. My life story, as it has unfolded since the events recorded in my 1994 journal, reflects my ongoing re-creation. In this span of time, my pursuit of life has been as dauntless as life's pursuit of me, and we are not finished with each other yet.

Knowing and being known are definite needs that we all share. I hope sharing my journal reflections—the directions they led me into, along with the story they birthed—will be of some value to the people close to me. I hope that they will know me better and know themselves better and that we will come to know each other better. I also believe that they will experience a shock or two as well. I certainly did, as I discovered that, after all, it was not just the early traumas that formed the core of my life's journey.

PART ONE

Excerpts from My Personal Journal, 1994

Pressing Grapes for New Wine:
Reflections on Religion and Psychology

Are we to understand the "imitation of Christ" in the sense
that we should copy his life, or in the deeper sense
that we are to live our own proper lives
as truly as he lived his individual uniqueness?
It is no easy matter to live a life that is modeled on Christ's,
but it is unspeakably harder to live one's own life
as truly as Christ lived his.

– C. G. JUNG

But in their rational selves, they shy like frightened horses
away from a God who is not the source of opium for the people,
but a reawakening and renewal of creation
and a transcending of the forces and nuclear energies in the human soul.

– LAURENS VAN DER POST

Excerpts from My Personal Journal, 1994

Day 1, 1994: Love Thy Neighbor As Thyself

Today it dawned on me that we began the Sunday liturgy with Christ's summary of the commandments. We've probably been doing it this way for a few weeks, and I find it odd that I have just realized this. The summary comes from Matthew 22 and reads, "Thou shalt love the Lord thy God with all thy heart and with all thy soul and with all thy mind. Thou shalt love thy neighbor as thyself." It is true that I see immense power in this simple summation, whose second part is, "Thou shalt love thy neighbor as thyself."

I have often wished the church would spend a decade meditating on this summary. After all of my own spiritual struggles and professional experience, I feel that these simple statements (my pen stumbles on the word *simple*, for they have immense complexity) plunge directly into the heart of my—and, for that matter, most—spiritual struggles and psychotherapeutic work, the work that has in its final explanation (as Jung noted) love as the healing agent.

A better understanding of this passage could lead me to believe that it is a call to a higher sense of self-fulfillment and self-responsibility. Then the term "led by the Spirit," which I have heard so much in my life, would have the full potential to imply a new *ethic,* one differentiated from the old simplistic code or conventional ethics. Such a new ethic, in my mind, would have to be steeped in personal integrity and understood in a new way, a way that is neither "Follow the rules" nor "If it feels good, do it."

The lesson on this particular Sunday continued with, "The fruit of the spirit is love, joy, peace, patience, kindness, generosity, faithfulness, gentleness and self-control. There is no law against these things." I think Saint Paul has gotten a bit lost in his own idealism in this sentence. This passage makes more sense to me when I interpret it as meaning that full fruition of spirit and vitality follow when we live life truly from our center, which is no easy task. But with this as a foundation, I am able to understand Christ's commandment to "love thy neighbor as thyself" in a profound way rather than as a simple

23

behavioral prescription. If I can love myself in the sense of being "led by the Spirit," then I must be able to have a full and loving acceptance of myself. I must first be very Christian with myself. As Jung says, my worst brother—my shadow—is within myself. I must accept myself with loving compassion as a first step toward my individuation and being able to love others. Once I can truly love myself, I am free—free to hear and follow the inner voice of truth that comes from the center of my being, where the immanent God dwells.

Day 2, 1994: Becoming a Person of Value

I am deeply interested in these reflections on self-love and look forward to continuing them. It seems clear, once I think about it, that if I am going to be able to give something worthwhile to someone else, I must first have something—something of value. (Whether literal or metaphorical, this statement is a simple truth.) Then, in order to have something, I must be a person of substance. I must, in Jung's terms, "consist of gold and not of hunger." Unfortunately, I generally got the feeling when I was growing up that most people who were preaching about giving of themselves meant that I should give of myself to their cause, their value structure, or—what is more likely—their need. Such people were usually very hungry inside and didn't realize it, which left them waiting to devour my vitality.

When such giving/demanding people gather, even today, I immediately feel burdened and judged. Subtly, or not so subtly, THEY put me under an obligation by communicating a secret psychic message that says, "We love you and you should meet our expectations." These people can be devilish. Yet the paradox of Christ's message stands firm in the face of this kind of pressure, if we have the courage to cling to it. I must remember to love myself first, to give something to myself, especially a life of my own that has depth and meaning. Then when I approach others, I am rich, filled with warmth and abundance and, perhaps, even challenge, and my presence is a gift to those around me. What a relief this insight brings, and how true it is.

Fortunately, I have known a few people like this, and they radiate

24

the richness and depth of life itself. Their presence gives the feeling of a large stone worn smooth by time and filled with decades of the sun's warmth. They have substance and seem surely grounded. In a sense, they are unmovable, refusing to tumble or be blown around by our frenzied pursuit of life. Eva (our maid, whom you will meet in Part 2) and my grandfather were like this. They radiated warmth, comfort, solidity, and shelter. They were resting places for weary souls, simply by the nature of their being. Such people also radiate a challenge to have character, values, and passions beyond the ordinary, to be so completely engaged in life that wisdom results.

In my case the proof of my substance is whether I can love myself enough to stand fast in the midst of a hungry culture, largely comprising people disguised as proper, loving folks. This is a hell of a problem for someone raised as a good southern boy.

Unfortunately, and all too often, we don't want to change. We like to think we have life systematized and explained. Then it is tolerable and seems functional. It has a meaning and a cause. Deviation from the "norm" upsets our illusionary system and threatens the structure we have built parts of our lives on. Well, we all get stuck here. The best I can do is to try and realize when I'm stuck. Life seems to have little sympathy for me when I am stuck in my own stubborn inertia and fear. Life presses on with the imperative to become more conscious and slaps me hard if I am blocking my own development.

Day 3, 1994: Self-Knowledge and Self-Hate

Whether I like it or not, I live by my perceptions, and this journal is the focal point of my struggle to sort out and through them in order to bring them into thoughts. As I work on these ideas, I hope they will combine into coherent insights into my true nature. When I reviewed the previous passage, I realized that if I am to be self-loving, I must first give up—or in a more feeling sense, sacrifice—my need and search for being affirmed by my loved ones and community. This isn't a "Which came first, the chicken or the egg?" sort of question; I must first make this sacrifice to become self-loving and realize that longing for affirma-

25

tion and admiration will be a continuing issue for me to be aware of and struggle with.

I have always found it tempting to want to do the right thing, the caring thing, and the expected thing in other people's eyes, to be liked, loved, admired, respected, and so on. Now that I have uncovered this fact about myself, it's not as enticing as it used to be. But once it was more than tempting; it was a compulsion, if not a way of life.

As a result, most of my so-called self-nurturing behaviors were really meant to keep the machine running: expensive clothes, numerous diets, exercise programs, massage, jogging, and the like. In retrospect, I hate the driven way I pursued self-improvement! I denied myself rest and truth, depth and aesthetics. I essentially "took care" of my mind and body in order to use them for the wrong reasons. When I use them for the right reason, they don't need nearly so much maintenance.

Doing the right things for myself is not the same thing as living the right life for myself. I can even conclude that living the right life for myself makes doing more of what I *think* are the right things for myself extraneous, if not destructive. Following this line of thinking makes it easy to conclude that more often than not, self-indulgence is more of an expression of self-alienation and self-hate than one of self-love. Oh, I like this conclusion. This equation is so true: self-indulgence = self-alienation = self-hate. I should write a book on this idea alone.

Those around us frequently want us to be a false self. They want us to be what THEY want us to be. I was a continual mystery to my father and stepmother because I was never what they wanted me to be, or even someone they could understand. My first wife went all the way through a jury trial at our divorce, trying to get society to make me fit her image of what she thought I should be. My children face the same quandary. Every so often they discover I am not who they think I should be, and a struggle ensues.

Think of the effort it takes as we are always trying to deny, conform, hold, and repress our emotions and behaviors to meet some covert norm that represents a "good" person. Without a doubt, to struggle against these forces while keeping in mind that cultural values are neither wrong nor unimportant (when on their proper level) requires a

26

tremendous commitment to self-knowledge. And honestly, self-knowledge, and only self-knowledge, can ground us sufficiently to enable us to discriminate between self-love and self-hate. This is the question I must face in each decision I make: "What is self-love and what is self-hate?" Along with self-knowledge, true self-love requires a passion for life that breaks through the smothering effects of conventional values and the desire for respectability.

Only self-love can support the moral initiative necessary to call me to authenticity and spiritual depth in my daily life. It is the foundation for keeping life simple, refusing to hurry, being aware of the beauty around me, and having the energy to fuel compassion and love beyond alienation!

Day 4, 1994: Obligations, Responsibility, and Self-Love

I believe I have reached a major insight in these reflections about self-love and self-hate. How can I tell one from another? The first thing that comes to mind is the word *obligations*. In this sense, obligations represent duties that come from outside myself, even though I may have made the choices that brought them on and may have even thought I knew what I was doing at the time. However, the more I think about them, the fewer of them seem to have resulted from authentic inner choices, a notion that doesn't and shouldn't necessarily free me of them. As I reflect on my earlier life, I see that too many of what I thought were choices were actually the result of desperately trying to be someone that I never really was.

Responsibility is a second word that comes to mind as I follow this train of thought. To me, responsibility seems more likely to come from within myself. Responsibility, as I think of it, doesn't just mean being responsible for the results of my behaviors. It also means being responsible for the origins of them and whether they are congruent with the purposes of my Self. It's funny. It seems like I should have always known this fact. Maybe I knew, but it appears that I never understood how essential it was to apply to the running of my everyday life, until my life collapsed into my second period of ashes at age thirty-five.

No one taught me—and I was late in figuring out—that the love of literature and the love of life must become one. Otherwise, as a reader, I am in a state of escape and denial. Of course, I often relished this state and used my escape into it to make my false life bearable. The experience of what I read and what I live must be reciprocal or both lose their reality, and I must ensure integrity between the two. Professionally, I call cultivating this kind of integrity "living the individuation process." Self-realization requires inner integrity based on the knowledge of our inner truth. In other words, it's damned difficult and complicated for me to live simply as myself in a manner that fulfills the pattern God has given me.

The more I can act "responsibly," the deeper becomes the well of my compassion, love, and abundance and the more dependable my toughness becomes when it is needed. The consequences of living this way mean that I can worry less about doing good works, for what is needed will tend naturally to follow, whether it is compassion or confrontation. But then I must ask myself, "Why is it so hard to live this way? Why have parents, schools, churches, and society in general declared living this way a sin and taken on the authority to impose guilt and shame?"

There is no doubt that my Self can be reflected only in what I do. If I am living authentically, the Self appears in my activities and accomplishments, and these always mean a relationship between myself and my surroundings—between subject and object. Yes, that's it! Once my actions are genuine, emanating from inside, then and only then do they show whether I'm truly growing and whether I truly have substance or not. Then I can examine the effects of my behavior—the influence I have on the world—as a method of self-examination, while being careful not to fall into the trap of valuing myself by meeting other people's expectations.

A lack of self-love can undermine even the greatest of teachings. For instance, in my experience of Christianity, I believe it can and has led to a profound misreading of Christ's greatest commandment—a misreading so profound that it reverses the field of Christ's message and the result is self-hate rather than self-love. In other words, many people have gotten it backward. I need to look into this misunderstanding more carefully.

A backward norm seems to have developed that we should practice charity (which isn't the same as love, because "charity" allows us to at least secretly feel superior) to our neighbor, first as a test of the charity toward ourselves. In this reverse manner, we will know our motives from our behavior and its fruits. Everything depends on our outer behavior instead of our inner state, which can only mean to follow the "rules." This attitude returns religion to being a law to live by, even if we don't use these terms. Religion then becomes a guide to social ethics. In this case, my inner life isn't a priority, and once again our institutionalization of spirituality has stolen the power from the transformative theme of Christ's life, death, and resurrection. When this happens, we are right back with the same problems of the Pharisees (who wanted all of the laws, written and unwritten, obeyed) that Christ came to transform.

My journey has taught me that I must learn religion as the mystics learned it, through the inward quest that Jungian psychology has helped me with so much. Banding together in institutions, whether religious, academic, or professional, helps some feel secure and able to look down on the unenlightened. But I've clearly learned that the inward quest must become one's own before it's any good at all.

As I remember the first three or more decades of my life, I devoted myself to searching out the norms of church and society. My attempts to meet them, to validate myself according to their guidelines, almost drowned me in self-hate. Trying to define myself by and for others led me in short order to become totally alienated from myself and God. But that God wasn't real at all. He was defined by institutional self-interests and concepts, just as I was.

Once I discovered that Christianity as I learned it promised something that it couldn't deliver, I tried other popular paths. First I sought the good life materially through business. When material success was no longer enough, I turned to humanistic psychology and pursued a more fulfilling life through personal development and self-actualization. While all of these efforts were helpful, their paths still seemed too shallow and one-sided to deliver either spiritual substance or a truly fulfilling life. Of course, a helpful guide to living Christ's two great commandments was never even on the horizon.

As I am finishing this reflection, I realize once again how different self-discipline and "willpower" are. Willpower—"take control of your life" and so on—seems to be our era's dominant superstition. Willpower causes us to fight with ourselves and struggle to resist or suppress our desires, thrusting them deep into an inner vault. Eventually, the vault becomes a crypt, stuffed with resentment whose passion will either periodically explode into our lives at unexpected times or slowly seep out, permeating the fibers of our existence. Self-discipline, however, sets me free! The discipline of asking myself the above questions keeps my deepest desires and values at the center of my life and passionately involves me in the process of living.

Day 5, 1994: Reflection and Self-Love

Reflection always seems to be the key to my self-understanding. But finding the time and energy for it isn't easy. To find a relationship with my Self, I must have the guts to step out of hurry and tension, center myself, and find some balance between being alone and being caught up in my life. It's worth noting that Christ followed this course. He repeatedly went into the desert, especially after big meetings and before significant events in his journey. First, he had to figure out who he was on his own, and then he had to unravel what his mission was. As his struggle progressed and he faced his period of temptations, I imagine that he also had to choose whether to accept his mission or not.

I never thought about Christ this way before. In spite of his night of struggle in Gethsemane, I never really understood that he had to literally choose much earlier in his life to undertake his mission and that this choice led him to his inner unity, to becoming "the son of man," a living symbol for eternity. Following this line of thought, I can see that Christ was truly human, and his choice underscores our natural yearning to be spiritual as well as the suffering this yearning gets us into. If I try to follow his symbolic journey, then I must, as Jung notes, try to live my life as authentically as he lived his. This is no small challenge.

And if I can discover and fulfill the pattern of life that is particular to me, then I am able to truly love myself in a way that allows me to experience abundance and the full fruition of life's encounters.

Now I'm back to reflection. Rather than theorize, I find it's better to reflect, to slowly chew over my experiences and emotions until I find a quiet ripening in my life that can be digested anew, giving new nourishment to the turning points of my growth. Slowly and deliberately, I find that I am able to see further into the people and events in my life until they begin to fit into a developing plot, a pattern. As I sink deeper into this self-knowledge, and as I witness its unfolding, I feel more at home in this world I was born into. The cast of my inner drama often surprises me with unsuspected faces from my past and present. Of course, the significant ones, as well as my own at different ages, frequently haunt me as I search to find their particular quality and understand them symbolically and chew the meaning of their images over until I can digest them as parts of my conscious self.

In spite of all of my graduate school training—which taught me to reduce, define, categorize, and measure almost everything that exists in order to gain an illusion of control over life—I seem to have little control over my own mind. I find my mind doing funny things with memories. It treasures them, and whether I wish it or not, my mind brings them into relationships with other things. Sometimes my mind does this with such intensity that I feel a force inside of me wants to design a new story from them or find some meaning beyond my sanctioned history and worldview. In other words, it is in my nature—and, I believe, human nature—to try and find meaning through the creation of stories. If I give myself the time to listen and reflect, my pattern will begin to emerge as my story takes shape.

It's puzzling, but I haven't thought about my own story in a long time, since my training days in Zurich. I used to think about it, or at least parts of it, daily. Now it seems not a day goes by that I don't think about my death. Perhaps I've missed a clue that I should have picked up on. Thoughts of death should return me to thoughts of life and its meaning and whether I'm living it truly.

But as I record my reflections, I have begun to see, hovering before me, my own face as a small boy. I find myself wanting to recognize him, to call out, "Hi, Buddy," and to wish him well in life. Yet it is already too late for that. Some would say he is no more than an electric trace, stimulated by some unknown impulse, stored in a brain with limited time before it rests inert. But I know he is there, and at times I wonder if others sense his presence. His countenance reminds me of life's cruel struggles and the eternal potential hidden within us. His image calls me to a renewed sense of vitality for the realization of fresh possibilities. Because I know his story, I know the pain inherent in this process—and the joy of fulfillment to which it can lead.

Day 6, 1994: Rediscovering a Life

My lectures and practice have made it clear to me that stories bring a sense of healing cohesion to life. I've found that no matter how much I study them and their archetypal nature or clinical use, I still think of them as being told around a flaming hearth or an open campfire. Storytelling seems best in these circumstances, at night, inviting communion around a warm fire as we are surrounded by the dark. I am now about to wander off into one of my lectures about stories. Do I need to hear it, or am I trying to escape something? I know stories transform us by exposing us to the elemental patterns of life, and they remind us that we are defined by crisis and conflict and not by happiness.

Could it be that I am reluctant to admit that I may have lost touch with my story—that I need to search for its thread, to re-remember it yet again? One thing I had better accept is that if I hear a story knocking at the door of my consciousness, I'd better switch my commitment from journaling to assisting its emergence. I know that its form and imagery will help me hone my experiences in a manner that will contribute to the heart of my self-understanding. The scenes will flash before my eyes like an old newsreel. "Is the story true? Is it factually correct?" the inner professor asks. These questions are beside the point—I learned long ago that the history of my life changes as I change. The facts are really bits and pieces of life that I am trying to assemble into a picture that I am able to comprehend.

32

I am glad I have the time to immerse myself again in this adventure. Suddenly my two cats have awakened and are tearing around the room after each other. Do they sense my tension and excitement?

PART TWO

The "Cracking Open" Story (1972) and Journal Reflections (1994) About the Story

The symbol and the images in which this greater Self pursued us, were always more than any dogma, theory or imagination could express. The answers it sought had to be lived before they could be known...
For creation was growth, slow, patient, enduring and endless.
There were no short cuts to it.

— LAURENS VAN DER POST

(Note: In these excerpts from my 1994 journal, I am presenting the story "Cracking Open" as it happened in 1972. Also included from my 1994 journal are my ongoing reflections about this story, as my memories from 1972 continued to unfold.)

1. THE BREAKING POINT:
Into the Shadowed Forest

When I had journeyed half of our life's way
I found myself within a shadowed forest,
for I had lost the path that does not stray.
Ah, it is hard to speak of what it was,
That savage forest, dense and difficult,
Which even in recall renews my fear:
So bitter—Death is hardly more severe!
But to retell the good discovered there,
I'll also tell the other things I saw.

— DANTE
INFERNO, CANTO I, 11, 1-9

Journal Reflections, 1994

I remember the first time I told this story, to Dr. John Mattern in Zurich in 1985.

The Cracking Open Story, 1972

Do you notice what Dante says about fear in this passage from the *Inferno*? "When I had journeyed half of our life's way, I found myself within a shadowed forest, for I had lost the path that does not stray."

Many writers about midlife have used his words about losing the path at midlife. But I haven't read a single one that pursued the profound meaning of the fear. Just thinking about these years of bitter fear stirs a chain of memories that began with the events of an early spring morning in 1972. I had driven desperately since the wee hours of the morning until the sunrise dissolved the morning mists in the north Georgia mountains. Having left a cabin where I had gone in a forlorn attempt to piece myself back together, I was headed toward College Park, a small town outside of Atlanta. My desperate energy reflected the erupting emotion that had been dammed up for decades. My emotions had turned on me as forcefully as I had repressed them, clandestinely consuming my vitality until the dam began to crumble. Their power drove me through the night into another day, through the darkness in my soul and closer, minute by minute, to the time and place of my beginnings and a story untold, a story I had violently denied.

Eighteen years earlier, I had lunged across the border between late adolescence and adulthood with all the energy I could muster. The intensity of my surge had carried me for almost twenty years. But my intense effort to be someone I wasn't, someone who didn't have my past, had begun to backfire, and my world was turning to ashes.

As I entered my mid-thirties, I realized I had no strength left to hope again for hope. I wasn't burnt out; I was wrecked. I was speeding away from the husks of my former ideals and ambitions, a spiritually bankrupt business, a broken marriage, and children who were scared and confused. As I drove, I didn't dare think about these things; I didn't dare think at all. I had failed in every single area of my life that I felt was important. As a result, I was driven by a need, which I didn't understand and couldn't question, to return to the place where I grew up.

As I drove, my thoughts traveled back through the years and through the darkness of an interior night. I clung to the steering wheel through the brutal fits and turns of mountain highways. Tears stung my eyes. I was headed home.

Shortly after daybreak I stopped at a small country restaurant. Thank God it was a real-people restaurant where you could get eggs, bacon, grits, biscuits, and endless coffee. After that pause, I was back on the road. I passed a little church, a white clapboard sanctuary with peeling paint and a stubby steeple. It sat, closed and empty, on short pillars of bricks. In front of the church, by the road, was a trailer sign with yellow lights on top and plastic block letters proclaiming: "WHERE GOD LEADS HE WILL PROVIDE."

Curiously, I felt better after seeing that sign, even though I hadn't been on good terms with God for a long time. I learned early in my life that he wasn't trustworthy, and I generally did my best not to believe in him. But this sign struck some psychic sense organ. As I look back, I know that at that moment an inner reconstruction had been undertaken by a carpenter so deep within me that my then-frantic consciousness remained unaware.

Journal Reflections, 1994

Now, looking back over twenty years, it almost seems like yesterday that I was speeding toward a standstill, a change in the tempo of my life, and a return to a place where the images from my past and memories would evoke piercing reflections. Now I can see that a new pattern was struggling to be born and to grow in my life. Its birth was driving me long before I could articulate it. Patterns like this one, born out of the depths that shape our lives, are urging us to look at them, and mine has become one that I have worked at and around for many years.

Today, I find it easy to diagnose myself. The wake-up call for my inner transformation and a new approach to life came as a crisis intense enough to separate me from the daily patterns I had immersed myself in. In other words, I had trapped myself in my own unbalanced perspective of who I was and what I was doing with my life. To deal with such a crisis effectively, I had to bring the forward thrust of my intentions to a full stop and travel backward in time until I arrived at a moment where re-creation could begin.

Psychology became the thread of Ariadne that began to lead me out of the threatening labyrinth my life had become in 1972. The chaos confronting me was breaking through the solidly reinforced walls of my identity. As the story of my return home shows, my deliverance began quickly, but it wasn't completed until it became a journey of its own. As this journey proceeded, I gradually discovered the power of our mythological past and how myths could help me discover structure in the experiences that I felt so lost in. This structure was immensely helpful in keeping me from drowning in a sea of emotionality.

In fact, Homer's *Odyssey* would become my *Book of Common Prayer* through this period in my life. Shortly after 1972, I was stunned to discover that midway through *The Odyssey*, Ulysses was required to stop and take a similar journey to the underworld—an underworld that symbolized his own unconscious and contained his origins and the shadows of the life he had lived up to that time. While deep within himself, he encountered the shade of his dead mother and a procession of ghosts of former friends, comrades, and enemies. These meetings grounded his present in the roots of his past, and from this point, he had to consult the blind seer Tiresias, symbol of his inner voice of truth, to discover the course that would allow his future to unfold. Ulysses's journey to the underworld provides a symbolic outline for one of the classic psychological patterns we experience as we mature. Once I had found a myth I could identify with, it became easier to see that myths could provide landmarks to help me navigate my own turbulent process.

Of course, in my frantic condition in 1972, I had no idea I was undertaking this special journey. Nor did I realize the helpful value of mythology or that I would soon encounter a parade of shades belonging to me. They were spirits of my early past, who had been left wandering in the twilight psyche of my childhood, searching for rest. Like most people, I had created a censored memory of my history that did not include these ghosts, and they were driving me to release them, to assimilate them, and to give them their proper place in my creation story.

I firmly believe that when we allow our outer crust to become dry and rigid, we invite life to plow us up. The inner quest, desired or not, demands that we be receptive and humble, and if we are not, life will humble us and open us up just as a plow turns over the earth. Then we are ready for the seeds. Or at least this is my interpretation of what happened to me. I suppose this opening up had to be. Like most people, I did not like what my early fears and hurts had done to me. Nor did I like how I had responded to them or the idea that they were continuing to haunt my adult self. In my 1972 crisis, life had taken me in hand, brought me to my knees, and was quickly reducing me to a state that was humble and receptive, a state that I had always resisted with great stubbornness because I prefer to maintain the illusion that I am in control.

In the underworld, Ulysses discovered that fate was not going to present him with the simple, easy life he desired. Instead, Tiresias revealed that his future would follow a difficult and complicated path. Traveling this path required Ulysses to carefully follow the advice of his inner Self, voiced through Tiresias, in order to avoid disaster. The path was extremely dangerous but led to maturity, relationships, reconciliations, and a previously unseen future. Well, I discovered for myself that this path to self-discovery and growth is fundamental to human nature, and I could not escape it. I must confess that following it has been painful and difficult, but it has brought me home to a wholeness of spirit that I had never dreamed possible.

Later when I became an analyst, I learned the past is as open to development as the future. To mature, we must often revisit it, because it is not something that is simply behind us. The past is the very foundation of our being. How we understand it and relate to it defines who we are and who we are becoming, no matter how much we may wish to forget it.

The Cracking Open Story, 1972, Continues

After failing to put myself back together in my mountain retreat and undertaking my compelling drive to the place where so many of the events that shaped my life began, I arrived just south of Atlanta in College Park. The College Park Presbyterian Church, the church of my childhood, became my first stop.

The clean, white-columned building that stood so strong and pure in my early years had grown gray and somewhat shabby with time. It looked old, and I wondered if its vitality had moved to the suburbs with the younger generations. I left my car at the curb under one of the large oaks and climbed the front steps between the columns, quietly musing to myself. I wondered if the transforming Christ had moved, too. Had he ever been here? Nothing, aside from my entire life, had ever seemed to transform here when I was part of its congregation.

Surprisingly, I found the door unlocked, and I entered the twilight ambience of the unlit sanctuary and took a seat on the back row. From there I could see the entire expanse of the large room. As I sat, I noted the arrangement of the room that hadn't changed at all, though it seemed to have aged along with the outside of the building.

My driven state of emotions ebbed and a total sense of lethargy embraced me. The sanctuary was white, empty, and starkly Protestant. There was nothing in this room to impart a feeling of warmth, no devout flames, no icons to remind us of God's active presence in the world, and no Christ on a cross to call our attention to God's knowledge of our own suffering. There was nothing at all there to inspire awe except my old childhood specters, which began waking up like the enchanted inhabitants of some forgotten fairy tale. Soon the church was filled with ghosts, my ghosts.

As their images emerged, I saw the forms and faces of friends and families, minister and choir. These were the people who had been prominent participants in my childhood. Over the span of my first fourteen years, they were present as the years changed seasons and as my life unknowingly approached a shattering climax. This church had been a vibrant part of the town in the days before suburbs. Six or seven hundred people had participated in its community, and now it was bringing back a thousand thoughts and feelings to me.

So much of my early life had been focused around this now-declining building. So many events that touched me had begun and ended here. My grandfather, pictured stern and regal in my photo album, had been a founding elder in this church. His daughter, my mother, had loved it. When she died, her funeral service had taken place here, ending my feeling of being at home in this building and community. As a child, I studied my catechism here and at the appropriate time had joined the church with my childhood friends. Later, as my mother was dying, while I was in this sanctuary, I had taken one of the first steps on my path to hating God because I felt he had betrayed all I had learned and all I had thought this building stood for.

The powerful emotions of family and childhood were divided between this church community and my home. My home was the other stage where the drama of my childhood was played out. These were two distinct main stages, but they were deeply intertwined.

✿ ✿ ✿

By the following weekend, the emotional wave of my return had crested, and I decided to attend the Sunday service in my old church. By that time, I was feeling more relaxed and curious and wanted to see how the church had fared. The congregation was much smaller than the one of my past and seemed to have grayed along with the building. I found myself in the midst of forty or fifty people. I believe I was the youngest, by at least twenty-five years. After the service ended, their expressions quickened, and their hospitality became so energetic that I later wondered if it was to cover their loneliness. As this group clustered at the entrance around the smiling, semiretired minister, I recognized Martha Berry, the old choir director. She may have been the only one left from my era. No other face could have touched me more or have been more precious to my memory of the old congregation. She was elderly, but she had retained her elegance and radiated vitality as she took me by the arm and insisted that we tour the church building.

I was surprised that I hadn't recognized Martha's voice when we had sung the hymns during the service, without the benefit of a choir. For as long as I could remember back in my childhood, Martha had directed the choir. In those days, the choir had been almost as large as today's congregation. I will never forget Martha's face as she stood alone and sang "The Lord's Prayer" at my mother's funeral. She sang in response to my mother's specific request, and her face seemed luminous as the tears streamed down her cheeks. Her voice filled the prayer and the sanctuary with beauty and emotion.

Martha had brought worship, suffering, and release to that sad occasion in a manner that was lost to me at the time. But somewhere deeper in my soul, it took root and has returned at various times to comfort me. I must thank Martha for giving me the image that had lay dormant for more than thirty years after the funeral. On this day the memory arose to help me see that beyond my anger, there had been a feeling life in this church, and there had been a time when I loved it and felt I belonged here. As I said, however, over three decades had to pass between her tearful solo and the time when I would finally let the same tears arise in me. We haven't reached that part of my story yet.

＊ ＊ ＊

I remember clearly that it was in the early spring when I was about eleven, a lifetime ago it seems, my brother and I were attending a Sunday service with a family of dear friends. My mother, sick with cancer, had become too ill to leave the house, and my father was too distraught to go to church without her. Our friends, knowing how important church was for her, picked us up every Sunday.

The seating inside the church was laid out with a large section of pews in

44

the center and a smaller section on each side. Then there were two aisles for the ushers, theater style, to show people to seats. A warmly paneled oak choir loft on the front left filled early with purple-robed singers. Martha Berry led them in the opening procession in her rich alto voice and continued directing the morning's music. Facing us in the center was the pulpit with three large chairs behind it, awaiting the arrival of our minister, Dr. Clarence Piephoff. On the right front of the church were two large double doors, slightly ajar, from which the procession of choir and minister would emerge as soon as the organist finished the prelude. Spring sunlight poured through the large, clear windows. The white interior and high white ceiling sparkled in a manner that was truly Presbyterian.

We sat about midway in the center section while the sanctuary filled with its community of families and friends, speaking to one another and settling down their children. Blue-haired ladies filled their customary front pews and fanned the pungent aroma of toilet water, powder, and perfume into the atmosphere, no matter what the season.

I have distinct impressions of Martha leading the procession and opening hymn that day. Her glowing complexion was enlivened by her kind, outgoing personality, and while attractive, her body was substantial enough to support the emotional vitality of her voice. In my memories, her solos were the central sign of emotional depth during the many services I attended. Short, stocky, gray-templed, and balding Dr. Piephoff sturdily followed the choir. He was covered by his somber black robe with his doctoral stripes on his sleeves. Dr. Piephoff, thoroughly Presbyterian, seemed German serious in his vocation. For a young boy, his voice carried the commanding resonance of his heritage along with its lack of humor.

Hymns were sung, announcements made, the doxology said, and the serious business of the sermon approached. For me, however, the serious business of my Sunday fantasy life was arriving. Drawing complicated battles of stick men obsessed me and gave me periods of respite from my sinking reality. So, as usual, I was looking forward to the sermon, when I could work in earnest without having to get up and down. I was observing the historical nature of Sunday by drawing an attack on Carthage by the Romans on the back of my program.

The heavily fortified city of Carthage appeared across the top of the page. Walls were manned by archers and soldiers. Up the left-hand margin, a column of stalwart legionnaires menacingly approached the city. Armed with short swords, shields, and javelins, they trod up the page. Before them rode their cavalry, accompanied by chariots full of Roman archers. Behind them, oxen brought up the catapults. Marching steadily behind the Roman eagle, they hadn't detected the ambush awaiting them. Behind the hills in the right margin, a horde of cavalry surrounding magnificent war elephants was poised for an attack.

"Whenever three shall gather together, their prayers will be answered," penetrated my fantasy as Dr. Piephoff's trained voice raised its timbre.

"What did he say?" I thought. He repeated himself for emphasis, and whether it is truly what he said or not, I heard, "Whenever three are gathered together, their prayers will be answered." It was as if a burning bush had spoken to me.

* * *

My mother, as I've noted, was dying of cancer. I don't remember when I first found out that she was sick or who told me, but I remember clearly when she sat beside me on my bed and told me that she was going into the hospital for surgery. This operation was the first of many. After that, as she got worse and her treatments increased, people told me less and less. A multitude of feelings come into my memory as I think back on those times, but back then I had gone into sort of a daze. It felt as if a heavy gray cloud had descended over our house, and we seemed to move in slow motion as its thickness oppressed us and obscured us from each other.

At a certain moment, my parents' eyes became somber and obsessed with worry. One morning I came across my mother quietly crying as she made my bed. I said, "What's wrong? Don't worry; I'll do it." She looked at me and, smiling through her tears, said, "I want to do it. I'm crying because I won't be able to do it much longer." I was ten years old and I didn't fully understand what she meant. The joy was gone from my parents' eyes, and in the evening my father quietly sat and smoked, waiting and tenderly holding my mother's hand.

I remember from earlier times the enthusiasm my parents had displayed as they greeted each other in the evening when my father came home. They would embrace strongly and seemingly forever. When I was very small, they would hold each other until I couldn't stand it, and I would try to break in between their legs. Then they would kneel and almost smother me as I was included in their embrace. I felt like I was in the center of the world where all was love and all was well. Sometime later, the enthusiasm had disappeared, and the feelings I felt were very different from the ones I had felt before. My insecurity was increasing. I tried to act as if it were not there, but I was afraid this awful time might go on forever. Underneath these feelings lay the terror of what I dared not even imagine.

I do not believe my younger brother and sister remember much about those times, for I am much older than they are. But I remember us all around the dinner table on Sundays. I had a napkin on my lap as my parents did. My brother's was tucked into his collar, and my sister's was fastened around her

46

tiny neck as she sat in her high chair. Before us were fried chicken, mashed potatoes, fresh vegetables, and cornbread. My sister held a spoon in one hand and a handful of mashed potatoes in the other, aiming it for her mouth. So you see, I was old enough to remember, to hear what the minister said.

❖ ❖ ❖

By this time, most of my mother's treatments were over, and she was home with two nurses dividing their time, taking care of her. Dr. Piephoff's sermon had galvanized me into action. I knew that with my brother and sister, we made three and we wanted our mother to live. Silently, night after night, I slipped through the house to their room after the grown-ups had gone to sleep. We joined our three sets of small hands, forming a tiny circle in the dark. We prayed, asking God nightly to let our mother live.

Bit by bit we were ground down, until we finally gave up. All the strength, comfort, joy, and vitality that we had known were suddenly gone, as if they were a rug that had been jerked out from under us. We were left dazed, hopeless, and exhausted. For me, God had betrayed us, and he was lost along with my other losses.

My mother lost her battle with cancer when I was fourteen years old. I recall sitting with my brother and sister, stunned and blank, in the second row of a packed church with a casket in the front. We sat between our red-eyed father and a solemn tower of dignity and grief—our longtime family maid, Eva. This was the last day that our family was together.

Journal Reflections, 1994

When God is lost, even for a child, all that is left is emptiness, whether we realize it at the moment or not. A restlessness begins to settle in and we become apprehensive. Deep in our interior, there is an instinct that knows we are standing on the edge of an abyss. Meaning slips away from us, and our way of life is endangered. The ruins of countless civilizations testify to this fact. However, it is difficult to be aware of this as it happens to us individually.

Decades later, sitting in the sanctuary of my childhood church, I experienced a haunting sadness. But no comforting vision, reconciling inspiration, or spiritual renewal was awakened. That would be reserved for a later date—another decade away, in another time of failure and ashes.

The rebuilding of my "inner cathedral" would have been scorned in the austere Protestant atmosphere that I found myself in. Reflecting today, I can see clearly that these two periods of ashes were connected; the second was a continuation of the first, which issued from the same origin.

The Protestant image of Christ that I grew up with depicted him in flowing white robes with golden-brown hair. He held his arms outstretched as he looked serenely at us. In a few pictures, he had insignificant little needle pricks on his brow and slight scars on his hands and feet. This image betrayed me in my most desperate hours. It wasn't able to support me during the tragic circumstances of my mother's illness and death or bring any sense of comfort or understanding that was worthwhile to my situation. It was simply too shallow and one-dimensional to have the strength needed to touch a boy or family in passionately failing circumstances.

In fact, the Passion of Christ had been whitewashed out of the mentality of my childhood church. Wine was reduced to grape juice; there was no stark Maundy Thursday ritual, no Good Friday service, and there was no Easter Vigil. Easter was a time for new clothes, egg hunts, and pancake breakfasts. Only the hymns were impassioned and violent. They seemed strangely disconnected from the people and atmosphere at church. Oddly bloody and pagan songs were sung by a congregation of supposedly good, proper, caring people.

So far I have encountered three transforming periods of ashes in my adult life. These were times when I failed and lost or walked away from much of what I had deemed important and essential. It was after the third period that I met the Mediterranean Christ—an image from the lands of saints and mystics, flame and earth, love and death. Here, spirit and matter are still symbolized in the eternal struggle to distill and sanctify each other. The churches, great and small, in this area reveal countless images, classic art wrung from the very heart of humanity. Christ nailed to a cross, slowly bleeding to death—this is the archetypal image of our transformation and an image so passionate that it has fired the souls of artists for centuries. I haven't found any other image of suffering anywhere that so depicts the human condition, the interface of human life and spirit and the meaning of transformation.

48

To sentimentalize religion as love and peace without the tension and suffering of transformation, in my mind, is to strike religion with a death knell. I found contentment with the Stations of the Cross, the archetypal steps leading us through the process of transformation. All nature evolves in this manner. But human beings experience this process personally, with a sense of "I" that goes through a psychological death before the rebirth of an enlarged and deepened personality. We know this process as one of torment and suffering. Transformation begins in pain, conflict, and betrayal.

The supporters of many Christian institutions seem fond of trying to see in how many ways, and in how many circumstances, they can ask the question, "Do you believe?" Whenever I hear this question, the image of myself as a boy returns and stands before me. As I gaze at him, I know this is the wrong question being asked to the wrong people for the wrong reasons. My questions since age ten have been, "Does God know? Does he know we are here, and does he know what we are feeling?" The answer from the suffering one on the cross—God in an earthly body bleeding to death—is "Yes!"

In this image of Christ, virtually abolished in our society in the second half of the twentieth century, I recognized the love or the compassion (call it what you will) that moved a dying Christ on Golgotha with a passionate power that reaches across two millennia. As this image began to fill the emptiness that had been created in me by my earlier experiences of Christianity, an inner reconciliation with my severed spiritual self became possible. Over time I began to understand that this image cries out, "God knows!" Then I was able to accept that people's suffering and struggle is sanctified. Such understanding and acceptance called me to marshal, from my depths, a force that demanded that I know God.

❊ ❊ ❊

Experiencing death at an early age thrust me into spiritual puberty, a developmental stage of conflict and struggle that lies between a simple childhood grasp of religion and spiritual maturity. With the normal flesh-and-blood response of my age, I, the boy, was appalled by a seemingly uncaring God and by the emotional stupidity of well-meaning religious adults—all those who attempted to comfort me with such statements as "Now she is with God" or "God wanted her closer to him." In a boy's eyes, it made God seem selfish and cruel. I had been thrust into a conflict of flesh and spirit. My mother may have been on a mystical path home to God, but platitudes could not fill the hole left by my mother's death. Her departure left us all emotionally bereft.

By the time I was fourteen, the church had lost me. I believe this happened because churches like mine had lost their heart and soul. This happened when they began floundering after rationalism and focusing on the externals of life. In our society, the "externals" equal our behavior. Make no mistake about that—the great denominations of American churches, no matter what their theological line, focus publicly on sin as external behaviors. The more middle-class the congregation, the more the focus may be termed "community" or "traditional," but the foundation is the same. As a result, God and eternity become impersonal concepts that offer little inspiration and less comfort to the human heart, which can be defined only by suffering and can experience joy only when fully open to the pain of life.

I found myself unable to figure out how to believe in either God or eternity. Of course, I now realize that no one else can figure out how to believe in a "concept" either. The rational approach to religion forces us to repress our emotions and deny any experience of spiritual mystery, which always emanates from the "nonrational" and can be known only through the symbolic reading of life. These repressions result in a denial of spirituality, or they are manifested in various idolatries, such as fundamentalism (idolatry of the word) or charismatic movements (idolatry of the nonrational).

My mother's death, my loss of religion, and the shattering of my family and feelings of love and security had left me a fourteen-year-old spiritual orphan. I became an emotional nomad, carrying a furious rage in my heart toward God, whose very existence I angrily denied. This mess still causes a furious rage in me, but I no longer direct it toward God. I've finally recognized the deep longing for God that it masked.

The experiences of our childhood become the parent of our emotional or feeling self. The feeling self that is part of us, the flesh-and-blood self, wants to live after death. I want to go on being who I am eternally—not to become a part of cosmic consciousness or some esoteric whatever. I want to see my loved ones again. I want to come home. I want God to care and to help me because—as a man of flesh, blood, and feelings—I have no rational illusion of control or power or even optimism. I learned of my frailty early. As a person of flesh and blood, I understand the advice of the disciple to beseech God, day and night—God, who doesn't answer but always answers. We are all flesh and blood, and to deny this feeling fact is to deny the existence of what is best, what is most vital, what is most truly human in us all—and what is best in God. I learned much later that to deny our flesh-and-blood reality keeps us from finding the true nature of prayer, which is listening. The serious part of prayer begins when our beseeching is exhausted and we can listen to the voice coming from within ourselves. And then we may discover that beseeching had a purpose all along and has awakened something deep within us that we need to stop and listen to. Whether we call it the voice of the Holy Spirit or the Self, it is always a voice that calls us to something new and unpredictable. Often, this happens through an unexpected demand that requires a change of self that will be both painful and energizing.

Today I think the agony of Christ, reflected in the great Mediterranean art, symbolizes the struggle we must endure in order to journey toward wholeness. The suffering Christ on the cross became for me an image of the anguish of the contradictory states of human life and human nature. I felt torn vertically and horizontally. To be whole, I discovered, we must be fully vital, passionately stretched between heaven and earth, the spirit and the flesh. And we must be broadened by love and despair. Vitality lives and is generated in and between these two opposites, both *contra-rational* in their nature. I have also learned that to understand this fact is to understand the foundation of our conflicts between reason and vital feeling, the mind and the heart. For me, the horizontal represents the linear perspective of reason: level, dispassionate, and detached. Of course, reason can be detached only by denying

51

the qualities associated with the vertical axis: flesh, blood, and spirit. When this happens, reason falls prey to its illusions of superiority. This image of Christ's suffering shows me that I must accept these contradictions for what they are and live by them. Simplifying my life or seeking peace in any one of the extremes then becomes an act of spiritual suicide.

As I reflect on the struggles in my personal history, I can see the importance of fully entering into the drama of life. Christ's peace is attained through the struggles and suffering that lead us to transformation. These were the cornerstones of his transformation: the process of life, death, and resurrection. His life reflects the archetypal pattern of how we grow, the pattern of life, death, and rebirth. This is a contradiction we have to live by. Whenever I tried pursuing peace on a shallow level, I found that my life became blocked until something eventually erupted. My studies in clinical psychology led me astray in this area, until I discovered what now seems like an obvious truth: Life is always a process. I do not live in the stages that psychologists have been prone to suggest. (Therefore, I have never been able to attain a stage of living spiritually. For me, spirituality seems to encompass the ongoing process of struggling to find personal meaning in the contradictions that life thrusts me into.) As a result of my experiences, I must conclude at this point that if I simply attempt to believe through blind faith or search for God through reason alone, I will have abandoned life; for I can be spiritual only through actively living.

Did I embrace this struggle when I was young? Certainly not. I've spent the last thirty years trying to avoid it. My return to the College Park Presbyterian Church and the childhood memories that rushed over me were a turning point in my journey back toward myself, but my journey did not the end there.

The Cracking Open Story, 1972, Continues

I left the church and headed toward a coffee shop. The power of those days around my mother's death surrounded me as if it had all just happened. I sat alone, drinking coffee and letting the past flow back into me.

The final scene I remembered from the day she died took place late in the evening. I decided to go out alone for a while, into the woods to sit in silence beneath the moon and stars. The night was very clear. As I left, my Dad said, "Go ahead. I understand and it is an appropriate remembrance." But I doubt if he understood. Escape, not a personal memorial, was my real intention. I wanted to be alone inside myself and avoid everything. Perhaps there was another part of me. Maybe this part was too traumatized for me to acknowledge. It could have been that something in my heart wanted to find a way to say, "Good-bye," or, better yet, to scream, "Come back! I need you! Nobody else understands me or even tries! I'm lost!" In the desolation of betrayal, shock, and not knowing, I was immobilized and sat silently, like a stone, in the moonlight.

Nothing else took place there. No peace came. No good-byes were said. No feelings welled up and no guardian angel came to protect me from the darkness. Perhaps I was stricken by emotions too big for a boy, but without her presence in my life, I felt surrounded by enemies. Slowly, without my knowing it, a large shadow enfolded me, a shadow of hollow loneliness gathered me in under the moon. I even felt estranged from the woods and sky—the nature that had once given me so much happiness and nurturing. So much vitality now seemed treacherous. It took me many years to become aware of the shadow that enfolded me that evening. From that point on, I began to live alone within myself, as if I were the sole survivor of some personal shipwreck. I was left with no compass, no direction, and no stretch of road before me. I was alone and fixed in time.

2. DARKNESS:
Savage, Dense, and Difficult

The waters surrounded me right to my throat
the abyss was all around me.
The seaweed was wrapped round my head
At the roots of the mountains.
I went down into the countries underneath the earth,
to the peoples of the past.

– JONAH 2:5-7

Journal Reflections, 1994

The day before I began journaling about the "Cracking Open" story and the observations it was spawning, I experienced one of those strange synchronistic events that often come with being an analyst. The last analysand I saw for the day shared an analogy, a small vignette from under the sea that reminds me of the hidden teachers that nature stations around us. Nature seems to wait patiently for our attention until she can help us realize how busily we limit our perceptions. Time and again, while banging my head against the wall of some issue, I have noticed that if I simply stop for a reflective time-out, some aspect of creation will gently step in and open a previously unseen door for me. Quietly, I find myself ushered past a formerly unsolvable dilemma. Often, as in this case, such help arrives as a pleasant surprise and an unexpected gift from the somewhat obscure atmosphere in which I work.

On this day, my analysand began explaining his own psychological growth by using the analogy of a crab's development. It seems that as a crab grows, its shell does not. Sooner or later, the crab becomes too big for its shell. What had once provided security and protection becomes a prison inhibiting continued development. When this situation occurs, as it does a number of times in a crab's life, the crab secretes a liquid that softens the shell and aids in cracking it open. Once the shell is cracked, the crab slowly extracts itself. Following this extrusion, the crab is vulnerable and must hide in caves and crevices until the new shell has formed and the crab is once again strong and secure. If it survives this process, the crab is larger and stronger than before.

Sentence by sentence, I agreed with him as he described how people seem to follow a similar path as they develop personalities, personae, and identities as well as the ego ideals that make up our value system. These aspects of ourselves form a shell that protects our interior life and allows us to operate more or less securely in our environment.

My analysand had discovered that like everything else in nature, people are encoded with an obligation to grow. However, unlike anything else in nature, we have the ability to choose whether we will cooperate with our growth or not. In life, our psychological choices reflect either our cooperation with or our resistance to nature's desire for us to realize whatever potential lies within us. Often, we resist our growth because of the suffering that is required to loosen the shell of our personalities and to begin the laborious process of extrusion from our old selves. Like the crab, we, too, may need to hide as we undergo these vulnerable changes, especially from the devouring tempo of an overactive existence.

Time and training have helped me understand the experiences I have lived through. When I drove furiously through the night in 1972, I was filled with self-doubts and self-rejection. It was an emotionally perilous time, and my sense of "I," or ego as we psychoanalytic professionals say, was in a precarious position. As it grows and changes, a crab has an advantage on us—it always keeps its identity as a crab. Because our behavior rests on a great deal more than instinct, our path is not so clear.

Shortly after 1972, I was severely bitten by the bug of psychology. I returned to school and read everything I could, wholly under the spell of trying to make sense of my life. I learned that in my youth, I should have developed a sense of "I" that would give me an identity and carry me through life's periods of psychological and spiritual development. When I delved into Jungian thought, I learned that my sense of "I" should be strong and flexible enough to both relate to the stream of life and express the inner patterns and potentials inherent in my Self. At the same time, it should prevent me from losing my identity or believing that my identity is all that there is of me. Boy! I loved reading about these notions. They resonated with me deeply. Just reading them gave me hope and energy. Two things that I learned during this time have never diminished for me. In fact, they have grown over the years. The first is a deep faith in life as a creative process. The second is the importance of approaching life through the process of reflection. This task requires an intense commitment, but it is only through conscientiously reflecting on my experiences that I have been able to see my true relationship to the world and the facts about myself and my life that are right in front of my nose.

During periods of transformation, whether from trauma or aging, our sense of "I" becomes vulnerable. In my own case, I had become

58

so lost and overwhelmed by forces from within and without that in 1972, I had to temporarily flee from my life. My depression, failure, and anxiety emphasized my lack of control in my life. I was forced to answer a loud wake-up call. It was a call from my unconscious, my Self, to become aware of what was going on beneath the surface of my understanding and transform myself accordingly.

Over the years, I've learned that after completing a period of transformation, we should feel stronger, enriched, enlarged, and more at home within ourselves and the world than we did before. When we follow the pattern of our nature, transformation unlocks additional bits of our future, bits we could never have imagined, and keeps us from being ensnared by our past. Armed with this information, we can easily keep in mind that the status quo is change, for we are continually in process.

From the outset, periods of transformation look like they will be devastatingly painful, and it is "normal" to resist them. In light of this tendency, I conclude that the more unconscious we are, the more we will need a crisis to wake us up—to crack the shell of the old life we are immersed in. Every day that I practice as an analyst is a reminder of how adept people are at creating illusions that help them avoid facing our reality and the transformation necessary for living a fulfilling life. We will try endless methods of self-improvement and surface changes until we finally manage to force our own backs to the wall. The story of my return to my childhood church in 1972 is the story of my resolutely hardened shell cracking so that transformation could begin.

This was a period that enlarged my life, but this enlargement required a separation from my old self and a departure from my old way of living. As my emotions drove me through the first night of my return and toward personal metamorphosis, I knew that there would be no return to my old life. Still, there was no comfort for me at that point because nothing could promise that I was headed for something better. If we don't manage ourselves deliberately, our sense of "I" may become inflated, despotic, and tyrannical when threatened. Then, unlike the crab who has no choice, we may make an effort to strengthen our old shell and refuse to leave it. Practicality, conventional wisdom, com-

59

mon sense, and caring for others are easily misunderstood and misused concepts that make wonderful excuses for cowardice and strengthening our shells.

No matter how well we use these concepts to avoid self-confrontation, in our secret hearts we know that we are betraying ourselves in doing so, preferring to remain under the hypnotic spell of our social conditioning. Under this spell, we can wrap ourselves in an illusion of safety. But nature is on the side of life, and living in this illusion can cast a dark shadow across our future. To maintain the illusion, we must place ourselves in increasingly cramped, emotional conditions. Eventually, despite our hectic lives, our pain may become acute enough to wake us up to how our choices have kept us stuck.

If instead we decide to redeem our pain and find meaning in it, we must confront it as if it carries a mythological message for us. We must be able to see through our symptoms and realize that they are the efforts of our unconscious Self, working to heal our personality and initiate us further into an authentic life. Addictions, compulsions, troubled children, relationship problems, and even physical ailments— both major and minor—may be wake-up calls to transformation. Of course, these crises may also open the door to a fear so great that it forces us to deny nature's imperative to grow.

On the surface, the consequences for refusing life's imperative to grow may be denied, repressed, and projected onto all kinds of other people. We find that society appreciates our conformity and confirms it with practical and ethical justifications behind which we can hide our refusals to grow. Our friends, family, and colleagues may even hold us up to be admired as "long-suffering heroes."

But make no mistake about it: Refusing to grow has fateful consequences. It poisons the atmosphere and people around us, causing, in one way or another, endless amounts of neurotic pain. Both Freud and Jung were unequivocal in their findings that neurotic pain results from refusing to face the suffering that is intrinsic in life and growth.

It is not an easy task to realize that our growth and transformation start with and include a process of suffering that we naturally would like to avoid. I was badly shaken the first time I realized the archetypal pattern of transformation begins with a peculiar form of suffering, one that is illustrated in Christianity by Herod's "slaughter of the innocents." At its outset, growth requires a death of innocence and particular potentials (symbolized by the male babies). This pain seems so unfair, and we feel as if we are the victims of an oppressive fate. But Herod has symbolic value, too. Herod, the old king wanting to stay in power, represents a strongly entrenched egocentric position that ruthlessly wants things its own way, no matter what must be done or compromised. None of us would like to identify with Herod, but that is exactly what we do when we refuse transformation.

After being bitten by the bug of psychology, my avid reading helped me realize that the mythological parallels to how we grow and experience life begin as soon as we do. While still in my student days, I learned that if things proceed favorably after birth, we experience a small symbolic Eden—a brief period of blissful nurturing in a protected circle of family life. This period diminishes as we increasingly join the world. Slowly we lose our innocence and naive idealism. Often when we feel overwhelmed psychologically, we try to re-create Eden-like experiences. For example, I lost my childhood state of innocence when hit with the harsh reality of the first grade. I checked out, withdrawing into a world of fantasy until a vivacious third-grade teacher noticed and cajoled me back into the classroom reality.

Those who miss this early Eden may spend a lifetime searching for it and for the unconditional love and affirmation it represents. While still half-baked in my analytic training, I learned that many psychological tragedies result from a person's insistence on remaining innocent and naive. We are born vulnerable, and our early experiences may make us even more vulnerable, even desperate and fragmented. But trying to stay in a state of childlike denial only invites further problems.

Curiously, our collective memories have failed to encode our complex vulnerability into our psychic structure. Each new generation enters the world peeping up at us with trusting, curious expressions filled with humor, vitality, and innocence. Conceivably there is a message here from life. Perhaps in our archetypal world, life can be other than what we suffer. Perhaps rebirth, as part of transformation, means we can cultivate a conscious innocence that cannot be slaughtered or altered by despotic idealism. Could it be this innocence is born in those who have struggled with and reconciled the contradictions of life until no part of human experience remains hidden to them and, in the words of T. S. Eliot's great poem, "...the fire and the rose are one"?

* * *

However, returning to my story of Cracking Open in 1972, my memories of my mother's funeral in the church reflect a time when the goddess of strife swept into my family, as unwelcome as the witch at Sleeping Beauty's christening. We were left as in a trance, to sleepwalk through life, encircled by an impenetrable hedgerow of shock and fear.

It was a time of brokenness that came too soon and too abruptly. Whatever had been left of our Eden was lost, and whatever remained of innocence, slaughtered. Our shells were crushed, aborting the possibility of transformation at that time. Yet in an inexplicable way, life also inaugurated the dynamics of a struggle that would compel my own personal odyssey and initiate a lifelong search for transformation. Into the ear of an already emotionally sensitive boy, fate whispered a destiny.

3. THE STREAM:
A Chrysalis of Bloodlines

Of all that has been written,
I love what is written in blood.
Write in blood and you will learn
that blood is spirit.

— FRIEDRICH NIETZSCHE

Journal Reflections, 1994

For this journey that I am calling Cracking Open, it was essential for me to go back further than the church and its memories. I needed to return to a more elemental time when I was still a member of a family, still surrounded by a household, and not yet split within myself—when I was still my own best friend and still in contact with the first spirit and primary ideals of my life.

The Cracking Open Story, 1972, Continues

In that morning in 1972, having driven through the early hours, I left the church after my first visit in over twenty years. Glad to be free from its haunting atmosphere, I crossed the street to a Shoney's Big Boy restaurant for coffee. The somber images awakened in the church faded as I sipped and my imagination returned to the present. I was taken aback by the realization that I had completed a passage. I had to steer my way through the shocking pain of my early life as Odysseus had to steer his way through the troubled waters of the Mediterranean. The search for my Self and a more authentic life lay beyond my early emotional experience. But a careful journey through these feelings was needed to reawaken my heart and open it to the task of bringing me back to life.

Then little by little, a vision, or perhaps a permanent memory, formed before my eyes as I gazed through a huge window at midmorning traffic. A miniature world appeared, a world of childhood. I saw several small boys playing amid a banistered porch full of toys, under the watchful eye of our maid. A tall gentleman with flowing white hair climbed the steps. Compared to the boys, he appeared ancient, but his eyes were dancing, full of strength and substance. Immediately the boys rushed to him. The maid smiled and he smiled back. Tiny hands thrust out, and he deliberately placed a piece of candy in each one before sitting down in a rocker to play with the children. At unexpected times during my life, this memory shakes me with the visceral effect this imposing man had on a boy of three. The poignancy of this scene quickens my imagination. I see the children loved, alert, and bright with trust and anticipation for life, and I realize it is a vision from my past. Strangely, it usually appears when my spirit is troubled. It never fails to soothe me.

This scene is the only personal recollection I have of my grandfather, my mother's father. Through the vision of this small ritual, I know how much he loved children. (One of my greatest fears is that our children no longer know how much we need them in order for our lives to be filled with love and meaning.) My grandfather gave me and the other children the small personal attentions that assured us that we were important to him, that he loved us and found joy in our presence. We grew up knowing, in our hearts and beings, that in this man's eyes, love is precious and life is rich.

My grandfather's presence comforts me, filling the hole created by my sparse knowledge of my family's history. He is an icon of kindness, character, and grave intelligence. As soon as I had sense enough to look back at it, this icon was there to assure me that I have a strong foundation and deep roots. As I mused over my coffee, I realized how deeply I had split my life, not just around my mother's death but also around my father's remarriage. After that, I buried my heritage in a forgotten inner crypt. I was glad to rediscover it. I hoped some of my grandfather's generative power was released as I opened its doors.

Journal Reflections, 1994

The hopes, dreams, and yearnings of previous generations flow into us, struggling against the tides of sorrow and disappointment. Blood-lines commingle, following the dark hidden knowledge of fate. Our ancestors honored the struggle of generations by placing churches and cemeteries in the center of town. Life grew from this commemorative center, as if to keep in our memories a living example that life can be transformed, but it can never be truly destroyed. Our ancestors and the dead are sacred because they hold the key to who we are. I belong to a society made up of people who fled their personal history. To find ground that supports me, I have learned to look inside of myself.

I have come to treasure Buddy, the image of myself as a child. He has never represented a "wounded child" to me, and I have not wished to heal him. His companionship is far too important to me for that. For better or worse, he carries the image of my origins and my hope for the future. In yellowing photographs, he is dressed in little football and military uniforms. He represents the pride and dreams of my parents, and his smiling face is not yet marked by life.

That morning as I sat in Shoney's, I realized how I had cut myself off from my childhood. This realization helped make me a student of those tender years and their place in our lives. The archetypal image of the child shines through in most of our early childhood photographs. These photos document that new life is always full of promise, even though we also know that many of these sparkling images cover sorrow and pain. Ideally, the presence of a child should call forth love, care, duty, and the promises of the heart. A suffering child demands compassion, and an abandoned child challenges us to face our responsibilities to humanity. Whether real or symbolic, images of suffering children have immense power. But too often we, as adults, deaden ourselves to this energy, for it calls for the kind of devotion and sacrifice that connect us to the basic sources of life and the meanings of the future. To touch this issue symbolically requires us to search for our true Self, our true life, and the best in the human community.

Children necessitate one-to-one personal responses—mother-to-child, father-to-child, and parents to each other. If we take symbolism seriously, we must make a similar response to the promise of our true Self and life. One of Jung's greatest achievements was to show us that the image of a child in our dreams and stories is the image of our own truest promise, and we must answer those images with personal love and devotion.

Various rites of passage mark the time lines of our personal histories—birthdays, graduations, marriages, births, divorces, joyous triumphs, and tragic events in great and small measure. But few of these events change the core of our personalities. Few of them provoke a true turning point in our story. The events and perceptions I am telling now are significant in the stream of my story. Turning points come when our old lives and our old selves fail us and our lives are blocked. The other collection of milestones normally used to mark a life, well, for me, they don't resonate at the deeper levels.

The stream of life flows into us in twos, originating in the joining of our parents' streams. This fact becomes evident as soon as our mental development reveals that we must begin evaluating things and making choices on many levels. From both streams, we inherit a complex mix of biology, psychology, temperament, and culture. These create a dance of images that shape our identities and our view of the world. Beneath this dance is a counter-dance of things we cannot see—including repressed emotions and unfulfilled desires. To be ourselves in our eyes and heart, we must know the images in this counter-dance as well as the more obvious ones. The way in which the images in the two dances embrace, love, hate, caress, fight, and ignore each other creates the ambience within our personality. These patterns of energy and experience are formed early and structure our visceral selves and the overall energy pattern of our lives. Our mother is the heart, internalizing and synthesizing the world without into the world within. Our father is the blood, circulating our participation in both worlds.

The Cracking Open Story, 1972, Continues

In 1972, as I sat in Shoney's with my thoughts, my coffee grew cold. Not ready to leave, I ordered a refill. Insights and memories were tumbling out of a long overstuffed closet, and I dared not try to shut them in again. I felt odd. This area of my hometown had grown seedy, though, and I was not the only strange character hanging out there. Buddy joined me. He sat across from me with a puzzled look on his face, a little ghost from long ago.

He smiled and listened intently as I told him how dearly I loved my mother. She was precious to me. I felt loved and understood by her in special ways that no one else has ever duplicated. She adored her father and how his values, classical learning, and awakened consciousness enabled him to pursue and fulfill a dream of life that was beyond himself. And yet she was reluctant to challenge my own father's dream for me, a fact that always left me feeling a little betrayed. They both loved me; I know that. I felt it clearly, and I can see it reflected in their eyes in the old photographs. But, as they were two, they split me in two, for they had two different ways of being in the world. Their differences were joined by a fierce love that was cut short too soon to mediate the split in me.

In later years, during my graduate studies, I wondered what my mother's destiny had been. Could it have been to love a man fiercely, to dream, to bring her children to life, and to imprint them with her soul in order to add it to the stream? Could it have been to imprint me with her father's spirit, haunting me forever with questions about meaning, character, and commitment? And what about her final years, when cancer became her spiritual director? Our most feared illness led me through what I now know are the steps of Christian mysticism. From the beginning, she had the makings of a mystic. She loved life, and we must love life dearly in order to be in a deep spiritual condition as we leave it. At first I wondered if some unhealed inner fracture had made

70

her sick and later thought this idea wasn't true. Her illness was an ordeal that caused her outgoing nature to turn inward, and her warm, generous spirit to turn profound, awakening her deeper Self.

Yet I continued to be haunted by her inability to confront her brothers, sisters, and in-laws over the cold and vicious conflict that came over the legacy of the school her father had founded. Deep wounds were inflicted in the family, and my father was one of the ones profoundly humiliated. I don't know what she did with the grief from these earthshaking events that pitted sister against sister and brother in a family she had once idealized.

Surely she suffered as she realized that she must give up her life so soon. The letters she left behind reflect her sadness and the grace with which she handled it. So goes the suffering of every person who follows the purgative way of mysticism and enters into a "dark night of the soul" that precedes a more profound spiritual experience. But her method of dealing with cancer was not bitterness, anger, or resentment. It was spiritual. I believe she tried as hard as she could to live, and she lived far longer than her doctors expected, while accepting her illness with a deep serenity.

As she proceeded through her ordeal, she crafted a sense of unity in her personality. The springs that fed into her became a river, and for her, its source was God. People visited her often and repeatedly. She gave something to life that was nourishing and whole: grace. For a few, it was too intense to see a person in her condition warm, smiling, and simply glowing with an extraordinary grace and an ease of mind. Sometimes when our everyday sense of who we are encounters the visible depth of our spiritual nature and potentials, it can scare and overwhelm us. The path she chose (or that chose her) made her illness a spiritual quest. This experience of transformation—not the fact of her illness, for I hated that fact—imprinted me deeply along with our community. Today that imprint often guides me as I work with suffering people.

As I looked at Buddy in Shoney's, I asked him, "Was it worth it, all that love and pain?" He can't answer me. He looks at me gravely through his eight-year-old eyes, eyes that haven't yet seen her sick.

The streambed of my life was shaped by my mother. Yet the echo of my father's spirit resonates somewhere deeper, if anywhere can be deeper. From the beginning I loved and feared him. Extroverted, passionate, aggressive, and competitive characteristics fuelled his full engagement in life and left him a storm-driven man. After my mother's death he sank, inch-by-inch, into a tar pit of loss, responsibility, and respectability, until the flame of his life was left smoldering and buried. He also died of cancer that began in his throat, and caused him to lose his voice. But his spirit—his fighting heart conveyed in words spoken and unspoken, perhaps imagined—are written in my blood.

The football myth of his era, with its grit and determination, was his religion, and it served him well. Football provided him with a way out of a poor family in a little Georgia town and into a small college scholarship and his profession. It brought him into a battling personal intimacy with life that carried him into adulthood and through the Depression, World War II, and my mother's illness. In midlife his football myth failed him, for times had changed. But it returned in his final struggle with death. His great disappointment was his failure, as a poor boy from an unknown town, to have earned a football scholarship to a large school that could have catapulted him to the top of the athletic profession. He dreamed that dream for me.

Before we had a chance to know each other, our temperaments had clashed. We never developed the capacity to sit down and talk together, and our conflict was never resolved. It became an archetypal deadlock between father and son. My father, like fathers throughout time, dreamed that I would carry his torch, especially the torch of his unlived life, into the future, but I had to live my life, not his unfulfilled dreams.

A key story in the Old Testament serves as a warning against such dreams. Abraham, when asked to sacrifice his son to God, had to learn to give up the very dream that his son would fulfill Abraham's unlived potential. This is the fact Abraham has to learn: What he is being called upon to sacrifice is not his son, but his own symbolic identity as Isaac's father—his dream of Isaac's being part of him continuing. The stream of Isaac's life belonged to God, and not to Abraham. In practical terms, this means we must let our sons and daughters find their true Selves and establish their life's patterns. We must give up wanting them to fulfill our wounded, false selves. My dad failed to learn this lesson, and shamefully I repeated the pattern. I hope I can at least help others come to this realization, as it is so fundamental to being a father or mother.

My father boldly leaped into the dangerous struggle of life, driven by courage and desperation. The sheer energy of his storm-driven life fueled his responses to the adversity and challenges he faced. His spirit of action and resolution filled him with a natural authority. Occasionally, even when I was small, I realized that he wasn't just what he appeared to be. Beneath his restless, stormy exterior lay a sensitive, intelligent, and fearfully vulnerable man, the complex man my mother loved so much.

The trouble between us—my father and me—was aggravated by the lottery of genetics. We were as different physically as we were in temperament. I was as introverted as he was extroverted, and I loved books instead of the competition of the playing field. He moved with the quick, short, stocky strength and the coordination of a fullback. I was large and slower. By the time I was in the third or fourth grade, it was clear that I was failing him and his athletic aspirations for me were becoming confused and distressed. We had very little in common. While he never articulated his disappointment, I have known it just as surely and just as long as I've known that he loved me.

This conflict, though extreme, was a traditional one. Certainly it hurt, but like many sons, I could have learned to live with it. What unhinged me was that I lost him twice. First it was to the dream of a son that I couldn't fulfill, a dream that was so strong in him that it terrified me. But the second time, the worst loss of all, was to lose him to a world of practicality and provisional living, to see his fire go out and his dreams turn to trivial fantasies.

After my mother's death, my father tried to reclaim his life, tried as hard as anyone I've ever seen. He tried to build a good life for himself and his surviving children. On one level, his efforts seemed to work. He found a "good wife" and a "good job." He provided well for us and truly contributed to the community we lived in. I still have deep respect for his efforts and how his love for his children must have motivated him. But, unfortunately, the secure, conventional life he aimed at and longed for became a prison cell from which he could see no way out. Like an obstinate crab, he hardened and hardened the shell of his life until transformation was no longer a possibility he could understand. Physically, he resembled the father I knew, but something inside of him vanished. His spirit lost its substance, its animation, and a large portion of its heart. He was no longer the man I had loved and feared.

Finally he heard a footstep behind him. His own cancer in his esophagus and his confrontation with fear approached. The night before his surgery, he stayed awake crying and praying. Of course, he told us this long after we could have had the chance to join him in this lonely vigil. Perhaps he finally needed to come face-to-face with fear alone. I think we all do. When he quit trying to live, it was an expression of a fact long past. By then I had lost respect for him. But I was wrong. He had tried as long as he could, and it was time for him to quit the trying that had become his raison d'être. He had remained himself in spite of himself, turning his final months into a fight until he exhausted himself, one final time.

Since 1972 I have wept for all of it—my mother, whom death stole from me, and my father, who was lost to something worse. Before then, I could not weep. The emotions were too strong and I was afraid they would overwhelm me.

Journal Reflections, 1994

From our birth, our mothers—but also fathers and, later, teachers, friends, and family—begin to teach us, to educate our minds. They say "mama," "daddy," "nose," "light," and so on until we begin to develop a mind that wants to name and order our experience. But as we form our identity and a view of the world, even of life, this ordering tendency can mislead us. Our minds, longing for structure and reason, insist that the inner world, the world of our unconscious, is flat. Our minds insist, in other words, that we have no depth and that half of all the contrary, conflicting dualities we run into, both within and without of ourselves, must be trivialized, denied, or projected onto other people. But the heart that beats through our psyche, as surely as the one that beats in our chest, never ceases in its hope to maintain the bonds of relationship with our inner life. The *others* we have denied and buried bubble with energy, like some ancient subterranean volcano, erupting into the ordered village of our lives with little warning. And the denied other—the attribute, emotion, potential strength, or weakness—who has been buried may arise, seizing and possessing us like some pagan spirit supposedly banished from the modern mind in which the inner world is flat.

This curious fact explains how all the characteristics of my father that I had rejected early on came back to possess my adult life. The shy, introverted son exploded into adulthood, driven by a competitive spirit and immersed in the courage to struggle and see life as a battle. This courage also saw me through some of my darkest moments, especially those crises that were spurred by another inheritance from my father— my fear and anxiety about security and money.

I ask myself the same question about my father that I ask about my mother: What was his destiny? Was it to be a coach and educator who initiated young men into a vision of life? Was it to imprint fierceness on me at a time when men seemed to have lost this capacity? Was his spiritual legacy one to compel me to attack life, to see it as a battle that would ultimately break your heart, no matter how brave you were? And what about fear? Must we hide it beneath the fierceness until it fills us with a devouring anxiety? And what about love and duty? Should they lead to a dutifulness that eventually erodes dreams and passion? What about God? My father was more passionate and vital before he joined the church (which he did shortly before my mother's death).

Like my mother, my father affected many people. Perhaps that was his destiny. He left me with as many tortured questions as answers, but he bequeathed the great emotions to me: courage, ferocity, anger, fear, and love. And he, like my mother, endowed me with an ability to imagine, to dream of a life beyond myself.

The other traces of my forebears are lost to me. To find out more about the dance of my inner ancestry, I have to rely on my dreaming self to bring what I need to know to light. To separate truth from falsehood in my life and what is "I" from what is "Not I," my searching, ordering self has to work together with my dreaming self. Thus, intimations of my true reality come only through a pair, a set of twos, a relationship of opposites that appear as contrary as heaven and hell in their basic nature.

The Cracking Open Story, 1972, Continues

In 1972, I sat dazed. Minutes passed and I didn't move. My coffee was again cold and Buddy had slipped away. What had been imagined and what had been remembered flowed together, leaving me in a haze. I was thinking, "We are the stream. We are the energy. And the treasures of life find those who are seeking them."

PART THREE

Excerpts From My Personal Journal, 1994

Remembering My Sessions with Dr. John Mattern in Zurich (1985-1986)

*He looked at his own Soul
with a Telescope.
What seemed all irregular, he saw
and shewed to be beautiful constellations;
and he added to the consciousness hidden
worlds within worlds.*

— FROM *THE NOTEBOOKS OF SAMUEL TAYLOR COLERIDGE*,
QUOTED IN THE INTRODUCTION OF
C. G. JUNG'S *MEMORIES, DREAMS, REFLECTIONS*

1. LISTENING TO GHOSTS

Fly, Holy Family, from our immediate rage,
That our future may be freed from our past; retrace
The footsteps of law-giving
Moses, back through the sterile waste

— W. H. AUDEN

Sad is the man who is asked for a story
and can't come up with one.

— LI-YOUNG LEE

Journal Reflections, 1994

(Note: At this point in my 1994 journal, my psyche surprised me. I was no longer in Shoney's. It was no longer 1972. It was 1985, and I was now telling my life story to Dr. John Mattern, as I had in the first of my admission interviews to the C. G. Jung Institute in Zurich. The scene shifted, just as scenes often shift in dreams. So, this journaling in 1994 became a story within a story, as if in a dream.)

Admission Interview Session with Dr. John Mattern in Zurich in 1985

"What are you thinking now? Is that the end of the story?" the elegant gray-haired man sitting across from me quietly asked.

My heart felt tired. "No," I replied. "Thinking of my parents always leads me to thinking about the lake. The lake was their dream, and Eva came with the lake."

John's quiet voice pulled me back into the moment. These were the first words he had spoken since asking me the question that had sent me back to my past.

His voice returned me to the present (1985), and I realized that I was gazing out of his window at another lake, the Lake of Zurich, as it sparkled in the September sunlight. Beyond the lake, postcard-perfect, the snowcapped Alps framed the horizon. This lovely view is the periodic result of a strange, ion-heavy wind from the south, the foehn, that sweeps into Switzerland. It erases the gray skies and opens mountain vistas. But restless nights, agitated days, and snarlish emotions follow this atmospheric change and serve to remind us that idyllic perspectives carry a hidden price.

My 1972 story had ambushed me when I began telling it, and it was persistently holding me hostage. This disclosure was my initial attempt at putting the events of my first and second periods of ashes together into a single telling. My effort had unsettled me as much as the foehn unsettles the sturdy Swiss. But in the presence of John's receptive humanity, I felt an urgency to continue.

I had recently fled to Zurich in 1985, during my third period of ashes.

By now I knew that reaching a low point in life was never as disastrous as I imagined it would be. But I had also learned that these times can reoccur and the suffering they bring is always hard to bear. I wanted to study at the C.G. Jung Institute in Zurich to learn more about these periods of my life and to penetrate far enough into self-understanding to find a reassuring foundation that would support me.

The gentleman with the quiet voice was Dr. John Mattern. John sat across from me in a comfortable leather armchair that matched the one I was in. John was a training analyst at the C. G. Jung Institute and a member of its selection committee. Becoming a Jungian analyst requires five or more years of post-doctoral training. Because of the intense commitment required of training candidates, the Institute is, or was, very careful and deliberate in whom it admits for training. Because of the personal and serious nature of Jungian analysis, the selection committee tries to understand the personality and character of candidates, as well as examining their other professional training.

My interview with John was the first of six that I would have with three training analysts in their efforts to get to know me well enough to make a selection decision. John had reserved two hours for this interview, which would take us into the early evening. I already knew from the experiences of my fellow candidates that trying to hide or put up a positive image would not work well in these kinds of interviews.

Before my first interview with John, I had already attended several of his lectures and found their intellectual content as intimidating as his elegant persona. Behind the lecturer's podium he seemed somewhat cold and distant. Tall and erect, he was in his seventies but looked younger. His casual clothes were well-tailored to define the contours of a still-athletic body that was accentuated by a long, narrow face. He had high cheekbones, a thin nose, and gray eyes that seemed bemused as he was lecturing. His voice flowed like a quiet stream that simply vanished when he stopped talking.

One-on-one, John was entirely different. As we spoke together, he relaxed into a total focus on what I was saying. His eyes brimmed with energy and his face revealed lines of kindness and humor. His voice now flowed deep with graciousness and became capable of leading and challenging as well as revealing his depth of understanding and emotional support. But most important of all, his energy and his intelligence danced and sparked throughout the room.

I realized that I hadn't answered him as I turned my eyes from the lake to his face. His quiet voice continued its probe, "You didn't mention your father's parents?"

"No," I replied. "My father's dad died long before I was born. I never knew much about him. I suppose that in my fantasies, especially as a child, he must have died to escape my grandmother. I knew her all too well, and she was relentlessly selfish and obnoxious. She lived into her nineties and my thirties."

My memories of her continued as I shared them.

❖ ❖ ❖

While I was a child, my parents referred to my grandmother as Mother Harris, and I thought she was an absolute brat. As far back as I could remember, she had lived with us, including through the difficult years of the Depression and World War II. During these years, her only contribution to our household activities was to wash the supper dishes. She stridently insisted she wanted to do "her little bit" and thereby condemned us to eating off partially soiled plates throughout my early years. Mother Harris never babysat and never helped with my brother and sister when they were born. At a later and more crucial time, when my mother became sick and she could have been of some real help, she moved out like a flash. Not wanting "to burden anyone," she deserted us and moved in with her daughter.

My father, having grown up in the South, stoically accepted her as a burden and never raised his voice or directed a harsh word to her, a problem he didn't seem to have with the rest of us. He used to say that she lived so long because by the age of sixty, every organ that could cause a potential problem in her had been removed. She and her blue-haired cronies would sit on our banistered porch, rocking, fanning, and talking about their operations until my friends and I would go inside nauseated.

Mother Harris, whose maiden name I no longer recall, grew up the only daughter of a rural Georgia minister. Apparently he considered every conceivable human activity a sin. This minister and his wife, who to the best of my youthful knowledge never existed because she was never mentioned in my presence, produced a daughter devoured by a fearful and frantic narcissism. Out of sight, out of mind, my father and grandmother must have thought, because they never spoke of my great grandparents. However, my father refused to set foot in a church until my mother was almost dead and he was engulfed by despair. Even then, the minister had to reassure him that it was OK to fish on Sunday.

Mother Harris frantically competed with me, my brother, and my sister for the family's attention. As the oldest child, I must have been the greatest threat to her, and we became deadly enemies. She would go to any extent to get me in trouble, often lying about my behavior and accusing me of insulting her in various ways. Generally, I was innocent of the latter because she was almost impossible to insult. But I made one early discovery that served me for years. Getting one of my friends to ask her how old she was never failed to infuriate her. When she complained to my parents that I had "done it again." They would respond, probably in secret glee, "That's just the normal curiosity of a child."

But not to be outdone, she devised her own means of revenge. When we moved to the lake, she lived in the guest room of the house. This room had a private entrance and its own bath. I slept on the screen porch that was left open during the spring, summer, and fall months. For the winter months, my parents had panels made of something called sun-ray wire that we put up. These panels were made of plastic-coated screen wire that kept out the wind and, supposedly, magnified the rays of the sun. I also had a small heater and was very comfortable, enjoying both the openness and separateness of this room. However, it had one crucial drawback. Mother Harris had to walk through my room to get to the interior of the house.

Mother Harris would emerge from her room early in the morning. Fully corseted against the day, she would dart birdlike into my room. Though she moved quickly, she reminded me more of a crow than a sparrow. Her darting speed made it easy for her to catch me with my pajamas off and my clothes not yet on, or vice versa in the evening. When I would complain about her intrusions to my parents, she would say, "I've raised two boys and it doesn't embarrass me a bit." When they said it embarrassed me, she would say, "Oh, pshaw." After all, that was her intention. But she had an even bigger weapon than embarrassing me. Whenever she walked through, she would "break wind." (We weren't allowed to say "fart" in those days.) She would emit the most noxious odor I have ever encountered at least twice a day in my room.

I complained vociferously to my mother. Mother Harris replied that it smelled so bad because of her "medicine," and therefore she couldn't help it. Desperately I beseeched my mother—my father immediately disappeared from such conversations—to require her to "break wind" in her bathroom. Mother Harris responded that it always happened naturally when she began walking, which unfortunately was about halfway through my room. My mother's requests went unnoticed, and I suppose she thought that a further battle wasn't worth it. But my resentment deepened into hate. Sitting at the ironing board and listening to these transactions, Eva, our maid, would peer at me over the top of her glasses and mutter with dark amusement, "Better thank God you live on a screen porch."

* * *

John laughed, reminding me that I was in an interview. But I couldn't help myself. I was reliving the story as I was telling it to him.

* * *

Later Eva would assuage my injured feelings with chocolate chip cookies. I often found myself caught in a duel with Mother Harris before I realized it. On several evenings, just when I was about to step into my pajamas, Mother Harris would spring through the door coming from the dining room as she headed for her room. She would stop in mid-dart, spin, and face me with a countenance that would have turned Medusa to stone. Thrusting out her finger, she would exclaim, "I know you put Jimmy Henson [or whomever] up to asking me my age! That's my business! When I'm dead and gone and you're looking down on me in my coffin, you're going to be sorry you did that." I would stand paralyzed, and by the time my churning brain cleared, she would have disappeared into her sanctuary.

❖ ❖ ❖

"How did you feel? How did you as little Buddy feel after such an assault?" John interjected.

"I'm not sure," I slowly replied. "I felt numb. I couldn't understand the venom. But I often thought, 'When you're dead and gone and I'm looking down on you in your coffin, you don't know how glad I'm going to be!'"

We never became friendly. However, as I grew into adulthood I slightly modified my perspective on viewing her in the funeral home. I became almost convinced that when I went in for a final look, she would sit up and say, "My, my, Buddy, it looks like you've put on a little weight." Today I find it sad that I have never missed her. Perhaps I should, but I don't feel sorry for Buddy, whose only living grandmother was a vicious brat. I feel sorry for the stress she placed on our family. Most of all I feel sorry for my Dad. I don't believe he received a single day of nurturing from her in his life.

Erik Erikson postulated that our primary task as we emerge from infancy is to learn to trust the world and life. Achieving this inner sense of trust depends on how we experience the ambience of our mothers. "No wonder," I concluded to John, "my father had a deep vein of anxiety. His mother was a childish ghost."

❖ ❖ ❖

In the interview with John, this reflection brought me back to telling him the story of how I returned home in 1972.

The Cracking Open Story, 1972, Continues

It was around lunchtime. I wasn't particularly hungry, but feeling that I should eat, I picked up some sandwiches at a local deli and decided to have a little picnic. I drove to the parking lot of the huge First Baptist Church, which was traditionally southern. In other words, it was a large red brick building with white columns, facing the main street. Even though it had been then and probably still is the largest church in town, the only person I knew that had gone to this church was Mother Harris. It looked just like it had looked all those years ago. I had spent many of my high school evenings necking with steady girlfriends in the dark recesses of its huge, tree-lined parking lot. On one side of the church was a playground and picnic tables. There I ate alone, quietly enjoying the warmth of the sun.

After eating, I sat lazily in one of the swings and drifted back and forth, enjoying the gentle warmth and serenity of the playground. I felt that I must be in the middle of whatever venture I was in and wondered if it would become second-thought time, if I would start to feel foolish being here. But no such practical reality intruded, and I decided to just drive around town.

The church was only a few blocks away from the oak-shaded grid of streets where we lived before moving to the country. The wide old sidewalks where we had played and skated were still intact. A few of the old south-ern-style houses with banistered porches still spread over lots with magnolia trees in their front yard. Some of them were as majestic as old sailing ships and they gleamed in remodeled colors. But most of the houses were sturdy red brick. On one corner stood a two-story yellow brick home with a circular driveway and a two-car garage that belonged to Dr. Davis. Occasionally, I would find that 1950s-style brick ranch homes with picture windows had squeezed into formerly vacant lots. After so many years, these stalwart homes seemed small and cramped to me. While it wasn't seedy, the neighborhood seemed tired, no longer enlivened by children playing amid the clutter of toys, bikes, and wagons.

I found myself wondering what became of my friends. Did Jerry Miller go into his father's dry cleaning business? Did Frank Martin ever finish Emory Law School? And how did Jeff Baumgartner's marriage to my ninth-grade girlfriend turn out? Futures had been far ahead of us when I knew them, and major choices were beyond the horizon. As I drove, I guessed that they were all still young enough for the possibility of a happy ending, but those thoughts did little to lighten my mood.

The vital landmarks of downtown College Park had disappeared. Proud stores and busy filling stations had either become decrepit or been replaced by low-lying modern buildings of brick and glass with postage-stamp parcels of grass and stubby shrubbery. The old brick medical building arrogantly survived and was painted a light, modern gray, accentuated by silvered win-dows. I was pleased to see that even though the commercial life had shifted from the downtown area, it hadn't simply become a collection of declining shells and boarded-up buildings.

The old yellow fortress that was the high school still hulked between the yellow garage-size town hall and the football stadium. Behind the stadium was a 1960s-style housing project that had replaced a run-down area of town. I had driven from East Chestnut across Main Street and the railroad tracks, onto West Chestnut. After touring the neighborhoods and musing for a while, I drove up South Main Street, through the center of town and out North

Main. I had never before realized how square and simple the layout of the town was, and I seemed to like that.

Finally, I pulled into a Quality Inn. I turned off the engine and rested my head against the steering wheel. I felt bruised and exhausted to the point of insensibility. Closing my eyes, I paused, listening to myself breathe. I knew I couldn't bear any more images from my complicated life for a while. Wearily I went in and registered. I was looking forward to a quiet meal, losing myself in TV, and delaying my discovery of myself.

I gave up on television, turned out the lights, and stared into the artificial darkness of the motel room. Outside I could hear the traffic moving toward the airport, until I fell asleep. I awoke the next morning, uneasy from a fog of dreams too thick to remember. I seemed to have been dreaming of things meant for me, but still beyond my reach. I felt that something within me had shifted and I could feel the return of a journey yearning for completion. I walked toward the shower, pausing in front of the clock radio, and noticed it was 8:00 a.m. I had slept ten hours and longed for a shower and coffee, the rituals that revitalize me before beginning a day.

2. LIFE SOURCE

I am black but lovely, daughters of Jerusalem...
Take no notice of my swarthiness, it is the sun
that has burnt me...they made me look after
the vineyards. Had I only looked after my own!

— THE SONG OF SONGS

And she, just like a mother quick to help her pale and breathless son by giving
him her voice whose calmness always reassures

— DANTE
PARADISE, CANTO XXII, 11, 4-6

Journal Reflections, 1994

1985 Interview Session in Zurich Continues

As I mentioned dreams and sleep, John's attention turned toward me with a concentration that seemed close to prayer.

"You had another look in your eye," he observed, "before I asked about your father's parents."

"Yes," I murmured. "I was thinking of the lake and Eva. Eva was the Black Madonna, the goddess of the earth, to me."

"There is a Black Madonna in the Monastery of Einsiedeln, at the other end of Lake Zurich. Have you seen it?"

"Yes," I replied. "But it is the wrong one. That one sits regally adorned, enshrined and protected in an elegant, spotless Swiss church. Besides, her features are white. She isn't heavy in countenance or body. She has no sense of soul and earth, earth made rich and black from the blood, sweat, tears, and bones burnt from people as life cries out for God."

"Are you sure you hate God?" John queried.

"Yes, for over two decades," I answered.

"But Eva, like my mother, had a mystical effect on me," I noted as I resumed my story.

I continued to live in two realities, the reality of the story in my memory and the reality of the interview.

❈ ❈ ❈

One of my parent's greatest dreams was to live on a lake in the country. Shortly after the war, they pulled it off, purchasing a lake and seventy acres of woods just five miles from town. The beauty of the lake enchanted them, reminding them of Highland Lake, where they were married, in the mountains of North Carolina. Eva and her husband, Horace, plus his thirteen children by his deceased first wife came with the lake. She was the cook and caretaker of the house, and Horace was the caretaker of the land, some of which he farmed.

Until yesterday I hadn't thought of Eva for years. Her black-skinned flesh was soaked with the qualities and wisdom of the earth. There was no *doubt that she was sensitive, proud, and stubborn. At the same time, she overflowed with a great spontaneous capacity for laughter, especially at the blunders of city people trying to live a country life. She carried the kind of weight that made her solid and powerful, rooting her to the earth and instilling her with a primeval energy and dignity basic to life. We all—with the exception of Mother Harris, who was spontaneously jealous of her—fell in love with Eva the first day we met her.*

As a White city boy in the country, I felt there was an air of mystery and deep strangeness, something impenetrable, in the life of rural Black people. In my middle-age mind, as I looked back in time, Eva's house was a temple to the earth. It was made of dark wood and stood on short columns of bricks, as many country houses in Georgia seemed to do. There was no electricity or running water. The inside of the house was dark and rich and always seemed to be filled with new smells and faces. Tantalizing odors of wood smoke, newspapers, kerosene lamps, and cooking blended. They came together forming a special, earthy incense. I love the memory of those smells and her temple. They remind me how sanitized I've become, and even though I prefer that, a part of me also longs for the mystical, personal nature of an earthier way of life.

When it came to food, I can say only that Eva could cook anything. Side-by-side with my mother, she raised and canned hordes of vegetables and fruits. And she baked cookies and cakes beyond the imagination. From frog legs to scuppernong wine, from turtle soup to blackberry jam, she seemed beyond challenge as long as she captained the kitchen.

Smart-aleck little city boy that I was, I first considered her a little ignorant and superstitious. She let me extend myself until this point of view was reversed on me. I still remember the first time this happened. It was shortly after we had moved to the country. My parents had bought me a David Bradley garden tractor from Sears so that I could help with the gardening and upkeep of the property. This was a very impressive piece of equipment for a ten-year-old boy. Proud of my mechanical beast, I arrogantly offered to plow up Eva's sizable vegetable garden for her. Formerly, her garden had been turned by enlisting her thirteen children, or Horace, if he wasn't busy elsewhere, had plowed it with the mule.

I proudly took the field with my mechanical beast. Eva assumed her typical boulder-like stance, arms folded, face quiet and serious. At this time she was surrounded by all thirteen children, who had turned out for this big event. Manfully I plowed and struggled. My machine, with the automobile-size tires, bumped and jerked over the freshly turned earth. The rows I turned were becoming increasingly erratic, but I stuck to my goal of turning over the whole field. Without moving, Eva gravely observed me the entire time. Finally finished and exhausted, I beamed, "How's that?"

She replied, "Thank you, it's fine. But if you had plowed in the other direction, you would have turned the dirt outside and on to where you'd already been. It would have been a lot easier." This, I discovered, is how you learn from country people. They watch you make a complete fool of yourself, and then everybody has a good laugh and forgets it. Once you learn to be humble enough to ask for advice, they generously lend a hand. Eva's practical, earthy wisdom represents a buried way of learning through experience and humor that has slipped behind our frenetic horizon.

However, there was more to Eva's knowledge than practical wisdom. She introduced me to a lost world, one that Dr. Freud and Dr. Jung had been exploring shortly before this time. Eva was the first person that I ever heard interpret a dream. This event moved me so much that I remember it clearly after more than sixty years. She came to work one morning and announced that her father, who lived a five- or six-hour drive south of us, had died. She informed my mother that she would like to leave immediately for his wake and funeral. My mother, knowing that Eva didn't have a phone, asked her how she heard about her father's death.

Eva answered that she had a dream the night before. In the dream, she saw her father walk down to the large springs, which were now covered by our lake. When he got to the springs, he stepped into them and washed himself until he had turned pure white "like an angel." Then he looked directly at Eva, smiled, waved, and disappeared. We were left speechless as Eva departed for south Georgia with Horace in his ancient Ford. Several hours later, we received a phone call from Eva's south Georgia relatives who were seeking to tell her that her father had died. My mother calmly told them, "Yes, we know, and Eva is already on her way there."

Dreams fascinated me intensely after this event, and we, Eva and I, often discussed them. Eva would interpret only her own dreams. The most

I ever got from her about one of mine was a sly smile. Once my mother became ill, she refused to discuss dreams at all.

❧ ❧ ❧

Eva wasn't above teaching my parents a few lessons either, and I still enjoy this tale from the past. During my sixth-grade year, I followed my peers into the 4-H Club. My first farming project was to raise pigs and the corn necessary to feed them. My parents had enthusiastically endorsed my venture, believing that we would both save money and enhance our natural food supply of fish and poultry. My father purchased ten little pigs, about thirty or forty pounds each, at the farmers' market and scheduled their delivery for a few days later in the week.

Enthralled with our venture, we neglected to consult Eva and Horace for their advice. My father energetically drafted Horace and me to skin some small logs to build an octagon-shaped pen about four feet high. He selected a spot near a creek for drainage and far enough away from the house to protect us from the odor. Eva, arms folded, watching us, gravely commented, "That sho' is a beautiful pen," and walked away. By this time, we should have known Eva well enough to detect from her comment that we were on a disastrous course. But we were too excited to notice her wry humor.

The pigs were delivered early that afternoon. While my father was paying the farmer, Horace deposited them in the pen. We hadn't realized that pigs are smart. Within five minutes, they had climbed out of the pen and were running excitedly around our back yard, rooting up our flowers and shrubs.

My father, aggressively assuming control of this fiasco, decided that we would put them in a small shed until we could rethink the pigpen. First, we tried to herd them into the shed. Our efforts involved a great deal of running around. By this time, Horace had quietly disappeared, leaving my mother, father, and me to handle the pigs while Eva observed. We didn't expect her to run.

Freedom and competition galvanized the pigs. Under my father's direction, we tried to run them into the shed one at a time. They squealed and darted with pleasure and not one ended up inside the shed. Finally, we

96

tried catching them one at a time. They squirmed and fought, with no idea of surrendering. After more than an hour of battle, we remained totally defeated.

We paused, exhausted, and stared at them. They ran happily around the yard, grunting, snorting, and seeming to giggle at us. I looked at my father. He stood breathless from the struggle. I felt the atmosphere slowly thickening with the tension of his impending fury. I could feel the inner governors on his rage closing down. Stunned speechless, I watched his eyes blaze with fury and humiliation. The primal blood of our ancestors throbbed into his neck and forehead. My terrified mother slipped into the house. I stood transfixed, frozen in captive attention, knowing that he was about to erupt into action and tear those pigs to pieces before my eyes.

In her usual boulder-like stance, Eva, unnoticed, had been observing this great tragic comedy from just outside our back door. At this point, she simply opened the back door and picked up the bucket containing table scraps we had been collecting for the pigs. A powerful laugh rippled from her belly. Without saying a word, but with white teeth and gold crowns flashing in an ear-to-ear smile, she strode across the yard with the bucket. The happy, greedy pigs crowded into the shed behind her. My father slowly sank to the ground on his knees. Then he began to laugh and continued until tears were streaming down his cheeks.

So, we all learned about the humor of nature, a humor that turned his rage to ecstasy, without belittling him at all.

❊ ❊ ❊

John sat quietly, smiling as I concluded my tale, but not making any comments.

I also felt compelled to tell John that there was an immense kindness and love in this woman whose heart was as big as her body.

❊ ❊ ❊

I never heard her utter a sharp or coarse word to a child. She would threaten, cajole, and bribe, using an endless supply of cookies that she maintained in the kitchen, when she needed to discipline us. As my mother's illness worsened, Eva's presence permeated the house, feeding us, helping us, and holding little hands against the mist of despair. She was a sharp contrast to Mother Harris, who skipped out. I don't know how she avoided it, but she rarely talked to Mother Harris. The few times she was trapped into it, she sloughed her verbs and became polite and unintelligible behind her Black person persona.

Eva's kindness and strength still warm me and her capacity for sorrow still moves me. My father wept for several days after my mother's death. But Eva's grieving started much earlier. During my mother's last year, Eva filled our house with a spiritual force. She prayed as she ironed. While moving about the house, she hummed the great southern spirituals of suffering and solace. When she was outside hanging clothes, her voice, which seemed to come from the center of the earth, would soar as she sung the soul-filled Black hymns that tell of a better life beyond this one. I wish that she could sing at my funeral. I would feel secure that her voice could carry me home.

It is through my experience of Eva that I understand our instinctual love for the Black Madonna, the Madonna of earthy people. Through suffering, she opens the heart to the wisdom and the majesty of life, while living in the world of everyday activities. She is the patron saint of abandoned children and Eva naturally fulfilled this role.

❖ ❖ ❖

"Hmmm," John replied, "Clearly, she brought a stability to the family, a kind of second holding, reflecting a primal relationship. But aren't you being too sentimental? Love, not balanced by authority, is dangerous. The two must go together. Unconditional nurturance or love, even in extreme times, destroys the soul. When we are no longer infants, it destroys our ability to develop our personality, and eventually, like Circe, turns us into pigs who simply live to be fed. What about Eva's other aspects? Can you see a bit of Kali in her?"

"Oh, yes! Kali, the Destroyer, the Indian goddess of birth, life, destruction, and death," I answered, recalling Eva's history. "She was fiercely independent, and got into several vicious fights with men. Early in her life, she killed a man

98

who tried to rape her and had served time in prison for that. Clearly she had another side that wasn't afraid of anger or even physical fights.

"As I recall her, Eva was a complete mythological figure. She handled death easily. If we needed a chicken for dinner, she simply stepped into the yard, grabbed one, and wrung its neck. When my pigs grew large, the vet came to castrate the boars we wanted to fatten in order to slaughter them. He put the huge testicles in my horrified hands and told me to take them to Eva. Seeing my stricken face, she teased me, saying 'Good eatin'!' Later, she supervised the slaughter and cleaning of the pigs."

John laughed, "What about sex? After all, you were in the country."

"She laughed and grinned when the animals and chickens mated. But there was another time that affected me even more profoundly. I was approaching adolescence and frightening things were starting to happen to my body and emotions.

"On a late Saturday afternoon, I ran into Eva in a dry goods store. I almost didn't recognize her because of the way she was dressed. She was in a two-piece dress cut so low that her gigantic breasts could have starred in a Fellini movie. Her lips were scarlet and she wore heavy gold earrings that matched her gold teeth. She had become the dark mythological sister of the Eva I knew, whose lush fecundity grounded a smoldering sense of sexuality. In this moment, it stood unguarded and she knew it terrified me. She laughed devilishly, enjoying the potent chemistry of a body exuding the power of nature. I felt overcome by dizziness and rushed out of the store, afraid that I would faint."

John laughed again. Eyes twinkling, he noted, "It's wise to be scared to death of the goddess, in whatever form she's in."

* * *

John was patient during my admission interview in 1985. He let me alternate between speaking and experiencing my flow of memories.

After a few moments' pause, he said, "You've encountered an interesting combination of mother figures. Keep going. What else do you remember about Eva? How does her story wind up?"

"Not well, not well at all. The last image of Eva that sticks in my mind came years later, when I was almost grown. My father had remarried and my stepmother ran a proper household. We lived in town, of course, where she/we could maintain her social status. One night as I was leaving for a date, I walked through our back hallway toward the door and saw Eva in the kitchen. She was wearing a blue uniform with a white collar and was peering through gold wire-rimmed glasses at a cookbook she could barely read. In our new life, she was required to prepare meals from a practical weekly plan and by prescribed recipes. Our cuisine had been reduced from wonderful to practical and mediocre.

"The mystery had fled from our lives. Instead of caring for animals, playing in the woods, and swimming in the lake, we led a carefully scheduled life of so-called meaningful activities. Today I despise that change but back then I was still too deep in shock to notice it. Reflecting on it now, I can see that with my mother's death, the heart went out of our lives, and we desperately clung to a life raft of social structure and respectability to keep from drowning. But in our desperation, as we betrayed the heart of life, we also betrayed Eva.

"You see, as I've said, Eva had truly been a mythological being. She had soul and she knew life. She knew it through her own experience: how bread is baked, how pigs are slaughtered, how food is raised and meat cured, and how quilts are sewn. She controlled her reality through the knowledge of her experience.

"Now our life had improved practically and materially, but she no longer had any control over her reality, and her spiritual essence had quickly eroded. I realized as I saw her studying there, patiently struggling to read, that she was now a 'maid,' in the true southern sense of that word. I didn't understand why at the time, but somewhere deep in my soul I was ashamed, ashamed for all of us. I left quickly, before she could see me."

"Ah yes," John replied, moved to quietness. "Modern life, how easily we forgot that we need the spirit of woman and her nurturance and responsibility for life coming out of life. Your story is very personal and poignant, but it also belongs to us all in one way or another.

"Let's take a break for a few minutes. We still have some time left and it seems at least one more mother figure for you to talk about."

3. THE WALLS OF JOB:
A Life That Works

*This man was indeed a man of mark
among all the people of the East
…So Yahweh asked him, "Did you notice my servant Job?
There is no one like him on the earth,
a sound and honest man who fears God and shuns evil."
"Yes," Satan said, "but Job is not God-fearing for nothing, is he?
Have you not put a wall round him and his house and all his domain?
But stretch out your hand and lay a finger on his possessions:
I warrant you, he will curse you to your face."*

— JOB

Journal Reflections, 1994

1985 Interview Session in Zurich Continues

While John slipped into the small kitchen next to his office to put the coffee on, I stood up and stretched. I walked over to the wall of windows and stared out over the lake at the sun setting behind the mountains. It felt good to move around, to breathe, to be back in the present and back in my body.

John returned with the coffee, in delicate china cups with a silver cream-and-sugar set on an ebony tray. Before sitting back down, he excused himself and headed for the bathroom down the hall. I retreated to my chair, where I found myself engulfed in the glow of the sunset, the aroma of rich Swiss coffee, and the old leather of the chairs—and engulfed again in memories.

I don't remember when my father met Ruth or when he told me they were getting married, but I remember being the best man in his wedding about nine months after my mother's death.

How did I feel? I don't know. Oh, I forgot I had stopped feeling by this time. I stopped that night in the dark after my mother died. I was sleepwalking through life, guided, I suppose, by feelings I could not allow myself to acknowledge. Their wedding took place in a small stone chapel at a mountain retreat center and, as a church, it didn't linger in my memories. An old family friend of Ruth's, who had recently retired as a minister, performed the ceremony.

I sipped my coffee, enjoying the sweet, creamy warmth.

"Going on without me, I see," John said.

I hadn't noticed that he had returned to his chair.

"Suppose you include me," he laughed. "What else is coming up?"

"I was thinking about Ruth, my father's second wife. About their wedding, in fact. I wasn't old enough to drive yet, but I was his best man. The wedding was performed by an old friend of my stepmother's, a retired Methodist minister. Many years later, they discovered that he had forgotten to file the legal papers for the wedding. I thought it was funny—Ruth living in sin—but she never saw the humor in it.

"But smile if you will, I agree with Dr. Freud. I don't believe the old gentleman was truly mistaken. Older and closer to the unconscious, some-

105

*thing in him probably sensed that their marriage wasn't valid at all, at all,"
I chuckled.*

"How did you feel during the wedding? Was it a shock?" John asked,
and blew on his coffee.

"I didn't feel anything. I had already decided that life was too dangerous and that I would sleepwalk through it. Of course, that wasn't a
conscious decision," I replied.

"It's been my experience," John said, "that answers like that aren't completely true. I believe you've thought this through a little more than that,
and I noticed on your application you were in therapy for a number of
years."

I felt his gentle challenge and noted that this was the first time he had
mentioned my application and its accompanying file, even though I was
sure he had read it carefully.

"I concluded in my earlier work that my history disappeared with his
marriage to Ruth. Quickly, the remnants of our past vanished. We moved to
a new home in a new town. All of my mother's belongings slipped away. I'm
amazed today that I have absolutely nothing that belonged to her, except a
few pictures."

John sighed, "And you didn't discover that you felt anything?"

"Oh, yes. I discovered that I felt a lot. I discovered that motherlessness
created a great emptiness, and this emptiness created a great need for approval, and that need focused on Ruth. I wanted desperately to be accepted
by her. As a result, I stopped knowing who I was. No, that's not true. I'd
already lost touch with that. No, I began a pattern of trying to please, to be
approved, to be accepted, to be safe. You know what I mean."

"Yes," his warm voice replied. "I know, I know. But I also know what
a dangerous path that is and how difficult it is to struggle back from it.
Nothing is more terrifying than the feeling deep in our souls that we don't
know ourselves and that the people closest to us don't know us."

"I discovered even more in my therapy. I had invented a history, a history of a good childhood and a family that was identified with success and
accomplishment. I was the grandson of a distinguished man. My father was
well-known and successful in our community, and my mother had been
inspirational and admired. Ruth's husband had been one of the town's lead-

ing physicians. He died in his forties, leaving her a large home and much of the downtown business district. I had the excellent makings of a cover story. And I began to live as if these ideas were everything. My grades improved, and my achievements soared. I worked like hell without even being aware that Ruth never seemed to notice, until no one in my family came to my high school graduation, where I had achieved top honors."

John made a slight sound as if to cough or clear his throat, but he didn't speak.

I slowly finished my coffee and put the cup back on the tray, afraid that if I held on to it, I might accidentally crush it in my hands. I was thinking that John is a wise man, perhaps from sitting on his side of the room for years, listening to one story after another until they became thousands, perhaps a river.

He cut off my reverie, asking, "What was she like?"

"What was she like?" I thought. "The question reminds me of one that an elderly, charismatic Episcopal priest asked me years ago. I had gone to his church with a woman friend shortly after my divorce, because we had heard of his reputation for kindness and wisdom.

"As we were filing out of the church in the line of worshippers, he stood at the door, shaking hands. I took his hand, introducing myself and my friend, and said, 'How are you?'

"'No,' he answered, his old head wobbling. 'How are you? How are you really?'

"I thought, 'F___ you. If I knew how I was, which I don't, do you think I would stand here in a line of people, telling you?' But I answered, 'Better. Better than I was,' and walked away."

John's face strengthened and his voice issued out with subtle power. "Are you telling me to f___ off?"

I realized I had been recalling the story out loud. "No, no. It's hard for me to think of Ruth these days. It pisses me off. I was so asleep, so scared, and trying so desperately to be accepted. It took me twenty-five years and therapy to realize that after all that damned trying, I didn't even know if she liked me. She had never called me on the phone to say hello or to see how were things going. I had an awful time in college. For several years my grades were bad, and I know I stayed drunk for at least two years. Never a word from home. Frantically trying to get a grip on my life, I got married. Never a word, never a call from Ruth.

"Throughout the years when I was struggling, when my son was in the hospital, never a call. Do you think she was there when my wife had her breakdown? Of course not. She never even knew about it. She never asked how we were doing. We were expected to call them, to go to see them. Of course, since I was always seeking approval, I didn't say much negative. The few times I did, it seemed to die in front of us, smothered under a few platitudes. She and my father made no effort at all to know me or my family or what our lives were really about."

My voice had sunk to a whisper.

"What was she like?"

"I don't know. I never knew. She didn't let anyone know, least of all me. I don't think my Dad knew. She was tough. That's what she was like. She was nice no matter what. She was tough as hell."

Silence settled between us until John's lights, obviously on a timer, came on. Even though they were soft and muted, I jumped as though I'd been stung.

"What was she like?" I mused. "She was proper. She was practical. She was propriety. Her appearance was always immaculate, always attractive, though never, ever warm in a sensual way. She never wore pants, except for the short life of pantsuits. She wore dresses and suits. Smartly tailored, expensive, rigid. She drove a big car and liked to give teas. She was dignified and she was kind. Nice. She was an asset to Father's position in the town."

"She must have been anxious?" John responded.

"Anxious? No. Or if she was, it was covered with steel.

"I had an aunt who was anxious. After the first time we visited her, my young wife said, 'We'll never ask them over for supper.' Amazed, I asked, 'Why not?' She said, 'Their house is perfect House and Garden, neat as a doctor's office, and she kept apologizing for the mess. She is as judgmental as she can be.' What my wife said was true, but my aunt was also anxious. My aunt wanted to be on a perfect stage.

"Ruth wanted to be in a perfect play. There is something else under all that; something they had in common. Hatred, I suppose. Perfection comes from the desire for a life that works, and this is a kind of hatred, a fixation

on form that denies the messy renewals of life. Anyway, we never asked either one of them over for supper."

"No," John challenged, "you are painting with too broad a stroke, and your answer is philosophical. Be more personal."

My face flushed slightly. I had worked on these topics for years in therapy and thought I had a handle on them.

"Listen," I said, "under her influence…"

"Which you just said, you rushed into," John interjected.

"Yes, under her influence, we all became actors in a play that did our living for us. You know as well as I do that that activity and a life that works well doesn't mean that anyone is alive!"

"But you needed this safety," John said. "You needed propriety. You all did. You needed the safety."

"Let me tell you something! What do you think happens to children when a family vanishes out of life?" I was getting angry. "Of course we were in a panic, looking for a place to hide. We had been betrayed by life, by God, by everything, and we couldn't stop until we were safe!"

"Or," he said, "until the betrayal is transformed, or you have destroyed yourself in the process of seeking an illusion, which safety surely is."

I slumped back in my chair, realizing how tense I had become. I remembered my stepsisters, how they had emerged into illness and addictions, until their lives became ghostly dead ends.

"What's wrong with wanting safety, a good life, or a life that works?" John asked.

"What's wrong with that? What's wrong with that?" I exclaimed. "You're an analyst and I'm a therapist. You know as well as I do what's wrong with that! Anger grows beneath such a life. It grows until we are possessed by it and turn it against ourselves. Rigidity and resentment become two sides of the same coin. Rigidity and over-responsibility in parents create an atmosphere where their children can be individual only by being irresponsible, and this causes them to become self-destructive and to hate themselves. We are angry because we can only love death, because what has passed for life is really a death-in-life, which has names like 'the right thing to do,' 'responsibility,' 'duty,' and 'respectability,' which in this form are worse than death."

"Of course," John shot back, *"this is the state of a life that works when its underlying values are all provisional. But this isn't a debate or a lecture hall. Say something real."*

Again I sat back in my chair and sighed. My mind searched for recollections and the questions that had been closed in my heart.

Slowly I answered, "With Ruth, there was no personal response to any critical or personal topic. And my father, my poor father, he and my mother had loved life and tackled it with love, courage, and fear. They fought it and they loved it. After death stole her, all we knew was fear. He, like the rest of us, closed his eyes and we searched for a protective script. His volatile temperament didn't stop with my mother's death. It stopped with his marriage to Ruth, like it was instantly frozen by an icy wind.

"All the important questions—hurt, anger, sex, conflict, love—were never responded to in a personal or understanding way. When my stepsister got pregnant, it was never even discussed. We just lived life as missing persons."

❖ ❖ ❖

I remembered that this session was an interview and that John was leading and pushing me into revealing different aspects of myself in a manner that also seemed healing. My respect for him grew even more.

"We are psychologists," he noted, "and it is OK for us to acknowledge it. I sense that we both know that when parents live unconsciously and defensively, they will push their vitality into their children in negative ways. Then, their children will act out and find themselves in a wasteland of pain that may free them to find healing, or it may force them to take on their parents' attitudes, as they seek to avoid destruction. We know that the best thing parents can do for their children is to ensure they are living a meaningful life themselves."

"Well," I reminisced, "a new wind had swept into our lives, bringing a new attitude of iron-willed niceness, and that's what I'll always associate with her. Perhaps I made the wrong decisions in my efforts to adapt, but they were the only ones I could make. Perhaps mental certainty is more important to frightened young people than truth."

"Consider it like a fairy tale," John suggested, following a line that Jungians often favor. "A new and powerful queen entered the realm and transformed the king. The new rule was social conventions. 'What will people think? What do people expect?' The order of properness and appearances became the silent tyrant.

"And perhaps a tyrant was needed to hold the realm together after such turbulent times. Of course, such a rule makes emotions a dangerous truth that has to be buried instantly within and condemned in others to preserve the safety of the realm."

"It comes to me now," I went on, "that I never saw her weep, never heard her raise her voice in passion of any kind, and never heard her speak of her father. We were left with a feeling that nothing was going to turn out right and it rarely did. Life is tragic and that is simply the way it is. It's better to be safe and conventional than to be a seeker and a dreamer. My grandfather's image had been buried and forgotten, and beneath our new life, I remained haunted by a great fear."

I stopped. I felt like I was just repeating myself.

John peered at me over the top of his glasses and said, "I think you're too hard on her and perhaps a little melodramatic yourself."

My anger returned, and I said "No. Death followed death! In our realm, love left, hatred left, and they took real life with them. Only niceness remained. When Ruth was dying, I felt empty of gratitude toward her. Maybe she had saved our lives by stabilizing them, but at the same time, she damn near destroyed us."

"You give her too much power," John responded. "Your father was there. He had some part to play in this drama."

"Damn it, I know he did. But he didn't know how to fight niceness and a good life. When he finally retired at seventy, she wanted a good life of leisure, relaxation, and travel. But he needed to look ahead to a new adventure and couldn't find one. Well, he found it in cancer, and she continued her nice persona as she nursed him."

"You don't let up, do you? But I believe that as you pull your deeper past back into focus again—and you haven't yet—you will find new energy and balance.

You are right in one aspect, a provisional life centered in 'niceness'—a *southern ideal, so I've heard—does throttle the possibility of true laughter and true grief.*

"They are suppressed for the sake of appearances. No comedy follows tragedy, as it does in the Greek theater, because no tragedy is admitted. The spirit is never loosened enough to allow vitality to renew itself. These are the walls of Job," he concluded, "the walls of illusion. The illusion that a conventional life successfully lived can protect and fulfill us."

For a moment we sat quietly and seemed to realize simultaneously that we had gone a few minutes over time. I shook hands with John, and we warmly said good night.

I left in a trance. It was a cool, wind-bitten autumn evening. The sky was clear and filled with stars. I walked for about thirty minutes and arrived at a park by the lake. To my right lay Zurich and its busy lights. Across the lake lights twinkled on the mountain, and boats still moved along the lake, with green running lights bobbing up and down.

I was extremely tired. I wondered if all of my interviews would be so exhausting. Then I realized that they wouldn't. John had helped me tremendously. His experience, intuition, and kind wisdom had moved right into my vulnerability, and as he learned about me in depth, he had helped me heal myself. I thought that after I finished with him, my other interviews would go smoothly. And, indeed, they did.

As I relaxed, I realized I had mentioned my first wife's breakdown. I was glad that John hadn't pursued this comment, probably because of time. We were young when we married, and she was bright, filled with energy and a quick, endearing humor. By her mid-twenties, she was beginning a slow slide into schizophrenia. I have to remind myself that the marriage wasn't all hell. That fact is so hard to remember, that it wasn't all hell. My life became so filled with confusion, terror, and back-to-wall financial problems that it seemed like it was always hell. But there were dances in college and, later, business parties where her eyes shone. We danced and had children. Our son was born when I was twenty-two. Then, as I desperately tried to love my children and thrust myself into the adult world, strange events started to happen. It would take a lot longer than two hours to heal this period of my life.

As I sat looking out into the night and feeling as if I were in a fairy tale, I lapsed into observing myself. "What a haunted creature I am," I thought, "driven by fates in some form or another that play out the elemental and eternal themes of dramas, tragedy, and comedy—I don't know which." Then, from somewhere—far back in my head, I think—I heard a feminine voice say, "John was right. You are melodramatic. Go get a glass of wine and a good supper."

I didn't realize it at the time, but this voice was one I would later get to know very well. Jung would have called her the voice of my anima. But I didn't think about that. I simply obeyed her.

4. THE TURNING POINT

*The child within me refuses to let go of his grandparents
as the man I am refuses to be separated from his father. My
companion, my judge, or simply my guide, he never leaves me.
...Smile all you want Dr. Freud, but I was attached to my mother,
maybe too attached.*

— Elie Wiesel

Journal Reflections, 1994

After the Admission Interview Session in Zurich, 1985

I returned to my room emotionally exhausted and quickly fell asleep. Naively, I hoped my dreams would simplify the layers of meaning I had struggled through and arrange them in some sort of helpful order, but this wasn't the case. Or at least I didn't initially see the dream I had that night as fulfilling this particular hope.

I awoke suddenly with the final scene of the dream still before my eyes. In it, I was lying on a bed, peering through the darkness at a doorway. My sister was standing just beyond the door as flames consumed her. My blood ran cold as my eyes lingered on this apparition. She was speaking to me, saying, "Don't be afraid. It's too late to stop now."

I swung my feet to the floor, flicked on my lamp, and reached for pen and paper. Questions rushed to mind as I fought to retrieve the images of the dream in order to put them together and write them down. Any questions I had would have to wait. I had to write out the dream and relieve myself by giving it birth into the light of consciousness.

I recalled how, in my dream, I was running across sandy soil from one clump of tropical foliage to another. Japanese soldiers, helmets on and bayonets fixed, were pursuing me. As I saw them, I sunk lower in the foliage. Clearly they didn't know where I was and were searching through the jungle, looking for me. Sweat rolled off me. I dashed from one hiding place to another, stopping each time to see if I had been spotted. It must have been during the Second World War. The soil was brown and sandy, the foliage a rich green, and the sun was blistering down through humid air. I passed a dirty stream and a murky pond. The soldiers were out of sight; I must have been getting away.

The scene of my dream changed, and I was safely in a small cabin on an island, standing next to my bed. The sun had set and the room flickered in the glow of a kerosene lantern. I heard a small rustle, and as I turned toward the door, I saw a beautiful, sultry woman smiling provocatively at me. She was just beyond my bedroom door in the dark house. Raven hair surged over her shoulders, glowing darkly in the flickering light. Slowly, as my eyes devoured her, I realized that her legs seemed to flow in the form of a large snake. Terrified, I flung the lantern at her and stumbled, falling back on my bed. She was doused with kerosene, which burst into orange-blue flames, now the only light in the dark house. She stood there, raven hair ablaze. Suddenly she turned into my sister and was saying, "Don't be afraid. It's too late to stop now." The flames soared, but she didn't seem to burn; she simply seemed to melt. I awoke.

The stories I had been telling John represented a remarkable passage in my life. As I pondered the image in my dream, I had the premonition that another passage had begun. In the story of my 1972 journey, I had been compelled to search for something, and as you will see, I found it. But with this dream, I began to feel that something was searching for me, not a woman (even though this assumption also turned out to be questionable), not an intuition or an idea, but something else I would later learn that my soul was lacking. As the dream began, I was in difficulty, and I decided that it might make my life even more difficult to bring this dream into my interviewing process. I decided not to relate it to John during our final interview. I saved it for myself to ponder.

Journal Reflections, 1994

Analytic Sessions With Dr. John Mattern in Zurich, 1986

A year after my interview and having worked with another analyst, I began my training analysis with John in earnest. After a few sessions of getting reacquainted, he asked what kinds of reflections the interviews had stirred in me.

"Two themes took root and absorbed me," I answered. "I realized how it is always conflict and difficulty that force me to wake up. These are the only stimulants that lead me to crack my old shell and move toward a larger sense of life and to endure the suffering that sloughing off an old calcified self requires. I also understand why so many people need a good illness or family crisis to get started. I've lived that one out, too.

"The second theme I've been considering is my childhood. I thought that when I had worked through my 1972 journey in therapy, I would be finished with these issues. To my surprise during our interview, I discovered

that all the old figures and experiences could arise and seize me again. But something seemed different that time, perhaps more intense—more intense in some strange manner I don't quite understand, maybe more mentally intense or imaginally intense. I'm not sure. Instead of feeling possessed, I felt surrounded."

"That's why the childhood years are so important," John interjected. "They're the pattern from which we grow. They are the first key, though not the only key, to the mystery of who we are and who we may become."

"I think this journey backward, down the trunk of my life to explore the roots, released the commandments from my past again. All the unlived possibilities of my life that had been killed, lost, or denied jumped out at me like ghosts from a closet. The better selves that I could have become, the happy successful self that could have developed, it seemed like a stab in the heart just to see what could have been."

"I wouldn't go too far with that kind of sentimentality," John admonished. "You could imagine that steel needs to begin its tempering early, and I suppose that nothing can spoil a promising destiny quicker than a happy childhood."

"Well, he's definitely not mothering me in this relationship," I thought to myself, while continuing to say, "I also realized that the images of my parents seem like the stones of some psychic or interior gristmill. Their turning continues, moved by the stream of time, milling me, commanding me, haunting me, and, yes, comforting me. I'm beginning to realize they will never be gone. I don't want them to be gone; they've lived and shaped me far beyond the reality of my actual parents.

"For a while I thought I wanted to build a life of practical duty. One Ruth would have been proud of. After cracking open and my breakthrough, which I thank God for because Ruth was never proud of me (she didn't take me that personally), I changed. A new awareness that I couldn't articulate arose from deep within me. When it became strong enough to emerge from its inner chrysalis, I realized that I wanted to build a life that would not shame my heart. In other words, one that my mother would be proud of.

"And my father—I felt like a Judas for years because I didn't fulfill his hopes. But I've discovered that I want to build a life that he would respect and even understand. After all, I owe him for whatever indomitable

119

thoughts govern my quest for life. Perhaps it has been my quest to reconcile my father's and mother's presence in my nature, gaining strength from one and spirituality from the other and a love of life from both of them, to struggle to bring their best elements into harmony, back to life through the veil of grief that shrouded my beginning."

"The figures of your parents are eternal in a certain sense," John said. "Psychologically, we all have what we might call two mothers and two fathers. In the hero myths that we study so carefully for their psychological meaning, the hero always has a personal father and a father who is 'higher,' which is to say an archetypal father figure. For example, Arthur, the son of King Uther, was given by Merlin to a more common man to raise into adulthood, at which time Arthur would have to undertake his own quest for kingship. Likewise, we have a personal mother and an archetypal mother figure. Think, for instance, of Moses, who had a personal mother but was raised by an Egyptian princess. These myths and legends have a far deeper meaning than we usually learn. At first, our personal parents carry the archetypal images. They personify them and this fact gives them intense psychological and emotional power in our lives. But if we hope to have a life of our own, we must wrest these images away from our parents. Then when we are adults, our parents are no longer gods who require obedience, homage, duty, and obligation. They simply become other adult human beings whom we may relate to as peers. We may love them or not, according to how our history has transpired.

"Of course," John continued, "they have given form to the archetypal images that arise from our unconscious to meet us at birth. These images arise from our psychic depths, the collective unconscious. Goethe called this place in our nature 'the world of the Mothers' because these images are the creators, the matrixes, the 'womb' of all our experiences. The Great Mother archetype represents all that is safe, nurturing, and transforming, as well as all that is destructive, chaotic, devouring, and transforming. She is the soul of life. The Great Father, on the other hand, represents law, justice, courage, protection, order, and transcendence, as well as rigidity, terrible and destructive authority, violent moods, humiliation, and demands beyond our means. He is the spirit of life in its best and most destructive possibilities.

"It is OK, even natural, for our parents to continue to symbolize these *forces as they do for you. But we must know which is which, which is personal and which is archetypal. If we confuse them, our lives, not to mention our relationships, can get in an awful muddle, filled with bitterness, obligations, resentments, and parental projections onto all sorts of people and even institutions."*

"Thanks," I nodded. "It helps to get a handle on this stuff in a way that I can understand. But let me add," I continued quietly, "that at the end of my interviews, I felt a sense of inner harmony. Not because I'd rationally put it all together or had some flash of insight that made things fall into place, but because it seemed like the simple experience of telling and your careful listening and responses were enough."

Journal Reflections, 1994

Analytic Sessions With Dr. John Mattern in Zurich, 1986

John began our next session by saying, "I've been reflecting on our last hour and on your interviews. I wonder how you would summarize the mother figures in your story today? What are their traces in your soul?"

"My mother introduced me to my life's greatest benefactor, books, and, together with my father, the compulsion to dream and the commitment to journey toward those dreams as far as I can go in my life beyond where I began. Whenever I see her picture, I'm pulled into her eyes. They were deep set and could be loving, penetrating, bruised, and smoldering. They always seem to see through me and, in fact, beyond whatever is going on. She understood me and molded my nature. I loved being with her. She was the sea and the wind that later turned into a spiritual flame.

"Eva, bless her heart, had sunk her roots in heaven and earth like the tree of life. She was fire and earth, but I remember mostly earth. She had the patience, endurance, and sweetness of springtime and a direct relationship to life that I have to struggle just to approximate. She taught me that life had to be warm flesh, something that I could experience, smell, see, and touch, or all of my books and education meant nothing. Her life combined strength, dignity, grace, and humor. She was indeed a second mother to me in a very elementary sense."

"And she introduced you to dreams," John added.

"Yes, she did," I responded and continued. "Mother Harris, what a trip she was. She relieved me of the guilt associated with anger and hate. And through the ways she hurt me, I learned about the honesty, value, and cleansing power of those emotions. I suppose I must thank her for that. But I still don't like her, and I will never forgive her."

John laughed.

"Ruth, I suppose, seeing nothing beyond practically arranging everyday life to be as comfortable and respectable-looking as possible, brought me face-to-face with two of life's fundamental decisions. I tried the first, the choice to pursue a life of safety and esteem, and failed. I am now trying to follow the second, the pursuit of a more personal and intense road toward a life of my own."

"Can there be a balance between the two?" John asked.

"I'm not sure. In some way, the very idea seems dangerous to me, even though I once tried to endorse the notion of balance. Ruth epitomized the appearance of balance. She was sure about how to live this life and probably the next. She had an uncanny ability to banish or trivialize everything that was troublesome or any fantasy of change that might be creative, that might upset her life. This trait seemed good on the surface, until I finally realized that it banished vitality and trivialized transformation and dreams. Her secret rigidity seemed to raise an unconscious urge in her children to disturb her comfortably arranged face, perhaps simply to cause it to fill with sharp emotion. Their efforts, which became immensely self-destructive, failed completely. As far as I could tell, her appearance of calm restraint was buttressed by a will of steel that seemed oblivious to the human heart's raptures and torments."

I paused for a moment, reflecting, and then continued. "My first family was full of faces—loving, angry, sulking, laughing faces. In spite of our troubles, hugs abounded. In Ruth's house, no one hugged or mentioned love. Isn't that funny? I never made that connection before. Where was my brain? Love was like a child who'd died and whose ghost was haunting us, or me at least, in some unspeakable way. A hole that could never be discussed."

"You've put a lot of work and thought into this since our interview, "John remarked.

BUD HARRIS

"I've thought and journaled for days," I responded.

"Let's see if I can add another dimension that you might find helpful, a little lecture on theory again," John began. "As I've said before, the feminine archetype, represented by the feminine principle of life, aspects of the Great Mother image and so on, gives and supports life. She has two characteristic forms. The first one is referred to as 'elementary' and corresponds to the maternal, holding, childbearing, nurturing, and protective features that we generally attribute to the symbolic nature of the Great Mother. But there is another side to the feminine nature, an opposite one, that is 'transformative' in its character. This form of the feminine corresponds to images of Sophia, the wisdom of the divine and the eternal cycle of life. Goethe summed up this aspect of 'the Mothers' by describing it in Faust as 'Formation, transformation, eternal preservation of the eternal meaning.'"

"Yes," I responded. "Eva supported the evolution of this pattern in my life and thereby became a foundation stone in it. She stepped in and filled the elemental position, the need for nurturance in my young life as my mother, in the grips of suffering and death, stepped over onto the path of Sophia. Eva filled this role as naturally as Cinderella's fairy godmother stepped out of the imaginal world of the Mothers and into the emotional needs of Cinderella's story. Thank you, Eva, for we know that discovering our identity is very difficult unless there are years of trust and support in our early lives."

Looking satisfied at my response, John sat forward and thrust his cigarette at me. "Yes," he said, "but you must remember that the feminine and the masculine have to travel hand-in-hand. The father's spirit is just as important as the feminine soul in making a transformation creative and personal.

"In midlife," he continued, "as you discovered, the renaissance of the personality begins. It is the epoch when the spirit of life, the Father spirit, calls us to the discovery of our individual selves, to be born out of the matrix, the womb of our unconscious."

"Then midlife must have been the point that was ushered in by my second period of ashes, where I began to free myself from the quagmire of my childhood. In your terms, I suppose that midlife is a psychological age, a point and not an actual age."

123

"Of course," he replied, "even though they often fall in close proximity. But I also mean that having your own life demands generation and new birth as well as transformation and rebirth, and thereby life becomes not only renewed but unique and personal as well."

* * *

After the discussion we fell silent. While John was lighting another cigarette, I remembered the dream of my sister. Soon John remarked, "Your face looks troubled. Something inside must be still moving."

Then I finally told him the dream of my sister and her conflagration. I won't elaborate on our work with the dream, because it was too long for this discussion. But it was a dream that ended in transformation, the transformation of my anima.

John noted, "You should be studying her now in your training seminars and know that she, your anima, is the image of part of your psychological makeup. She is the feminine part of your nature, all that you can see and experience in a woman. Your experience of your mother is the first imprint on your anima, but she isn't your mother or any woman that you have loved or hated. Still, you probably see part of her in each of them because if you love a woman, you project part of this image on her, at least initially. The same is true if you hate a woman, because our anima also has a very disagreeable side. She inspires great art and poetry, compassion through love and endurance, wars of passion and jealousy, as well as some of our greatest love stories.

"She develops through several psychological and imaginal stages that are archetypal and have both positive and negative potentials. They are imaged as mother, lover, inspiritrix/creatrix, and wisdom. In our personal life, an additional image, that of sister, the sister anima, helps us differentiate from the mother stage and move toward the lover, the capacity to be in love with and then love a woman.

"In your dreams, we see you fleeing from an old and threatening inner conflict that takes place on an island in isolation. You reach the sanctity of your cabin, and when inside or withdrawn into yourself, you feel safe. And then your anima appears in the form of Melusina."

"*Who?*"

"*Melusina, a mythological figure, a nixie, a fairy temptress. She probably represents a wounded, undeveloped aspect of the feminine in you, most likely the result of your early life. I would imagine that she tempts you to lead your real life in a land of fantasy, not in the flesh-and-blood world, even though you may appear very competent in the outer world. Combining your history and love of books makes you an easy mark for her.*"

I was stunned, knowing that he was right.

"*It's a good sign,*" *he continued,* "*as she transforms into your sister. This step may help you toward realizing a flesh-and-blood relationship with a woman, one that I imagine you haven't had, in spite of being married.*"

Again he was right. My early marriage had marked a desperate search for manhood, pursued by plunging blindly into responsibility.

As our discussion continued, I realized that Melusina had rescued me from a struggle I couldn't face, though she had caused me plenty of trouble. Since my early life, an inner dance had begun between loss and fear, woman and death. Woman, love, death, and God had combined in a fearsome quaternity.

John's voice interrupted my reverie. "*I see we still have plenty to do, and our hour is finished. We'll resume our discussion on Thursday.*"

Journal Reflections, 1994, Selection

There is no doubt in my mind that the journey into "being" must be based on a profound journey into self-love. Self-love requires a deep knowledge of myself. Otherwise I am trying to love someone I don't really know. I learned a long time ago that loving someone I don't really know is simply a projection or a sentimental fantasy.

Just as John and I had more work to do all of those years ago, I see today that the work I'm doing here needs to continue. And it will.

EPILOGUE: 2015

As I have reflected on these pages from over twenty years ago, I realize my writing has always been a quest, a kind of pilgrimage. I am also aware that it has never been easy for me to make my private thoughts public. For every piece of writing that I create and share, I have to give myself permission both to write and then to make it public. As far as I can see, I am not alone in these circumstances. Permission to take the time and spend the energy to be creative seems to be a scarce commodity for most people in our busy world.

I find myself now many years wiser, reading these pages with affection. Several times my eyes were blurring. Was I becoming overwhelmed with emotion? No, but I was moved by how I struggled through change. I never intended to share my journal entries, but I see value in my experiences. These pages were written with hope, with love, and with an underlying intention. They elevated the pain and struggles of my past with the kind of compassion and understanding that enlarged and continues to enlarge my life. It was hard for me to comprehend all those years ago that time and inner work cannot heal all wounds. Some remain open and raw. But the Self—the central element in our lives and our Divine spark—is the architect of our personality and the carrier of the "blueprint" that can guide our growth. As such, the Self can, time and again, use our pain to transform us.

Throughout my years of Jungian work, which is based on the ability to reflect on one's life, I learned that reflecting also includes "re-membering." In the individuation process, re-membering involves living in more than one world. Re-membering one's life helps prevent the "past" from fading and helps integrate it with our present and future worlds so that all phases of our life—past, present, and future—can transform each other. As I re-member my life, I can recall, even today, the absolute devastation I, Buddy, felt when my mother died. Buddy believed that she was the only one who understood him. After her death, he was alone, surrounded only by strangers and enemies, including God. While I was reading about my father, I realized again how little I actually knew of his story and how much I would have liked to have known it better.

* * *

Life always seems to shake my inner peace. As an emerging elder, I have finally learned to overcome some of my fear of my encounters with these moments and events. Sometimes, I even desire them. More than three decades ago, as my work with my analyst in Zurich progressed, I learned that we are defined by what troubles us, and not by what reassures us. We often need to start some part of our lives all over again. Moreover, we need to face these moments of change head on with a courage that is supported by a love of life and energized by an inner quest for self-awareness and consciousness.

There seems to be no end to the kinds of things that can trouble us and trigger our need for transformation. Failure was often the trigger for me. Failure began early for me, when I started becoming aware that I was failing to meet my father's expectations of me. Sadly, in my early life I never gave myself permission not to take the road I was expected to take. Perhaps, trusting the expectations of influential people and forces in my life, I bought into their expectations for my life, making them my own. Failure gave me permission, sometimes brutally, to override these expectations and forced me to take different paths. Again and again, in my early adulthood, I seemed to succeed, only to hit a wall in my life and descend into ashes. Such was the case when I returned to my hometown in 1972.

I would like to think that I was a maverick, a dreamer, and a dissenter—one who lives creatively. Well, actually I am, especially today, but I didn't start out that way. I started out trying to climb the rungs on the ladder of a conventional adult life, which I did well and intensely until life knocked me off the ladder. For me, at any rate, taking side trips, wandering in different directions, faltering, pulling back, and starting over were usually initiated by failure. When I was growing up, in my crowd, failures in grades, sports, marriages, and jobs were considered failures in life. Parents, teachers, coaches, and even our priests and ministers made it clear: "Don't fail." So, failures tended to brutalize my self-esteem.

But as I recounted my story to John, my whole perspective shifted. I realized how my greatest transformations began with failure. Within a short period during our work together, I recognized that I had never been transformed or learned anything significant from success. So, now I look at failure as the first step on a new journey. My lifetime of experience reminds me of Jung's admonition that if we do the wrong thing with all of our hearts, we will end up at the right place. I look back today on my stories as friends, as mementos of my life's struggles that brought the rewards of forming who I am.

* * *

While studying in Zurich, over thirty years ago, I realized that there is a storyline, a pattern, underlying the events in my life. This pattern is carried by our Self. In Jung's conception, the Self is the "mysterious" entity that creates and sustains all of the life within us. It is an invisible power that acts as the creator and carrier of all of our preexisting, built-in patterns of behavior. It is the urge within us to live and produce life. The Self is the cause of our individuation process, and the Self is the goal of this process: a complete, fully developed person. Because it involves creation and re-creation, individuation is a life's work. It involves joining together conscious intelligence, the ego, with the greater intelligence of the Self and the instincts of the unconscious. Once this happens, a person is no longer split within himself or herself. The person is no longer identified solely with his or her ego or instinctual, unconscious impulses and complexes. For me, individuation helped me transcend my ego and unconscious drives. The process enlarged my consciousness and ability to live at home in the pattern of my life as contained in the Self.

* * *

While I was struggling to understand and assimilate the complexities of Jung's theories at the Jung Institute, I was also working in my analysis with John to live and experience the journey of individuation that Jung so profoundly explains. It didn't take long for me to figure out that individuation is a lifelong journey, not a destination, and that pursuing it made me feel myself becoming more fully alive, more than I had ever imagined possible.

My journal entries document key moments and phases in my individuation. Part 1 of this book records my ongoing spiritual and religious quest, my attempt to find meaning in spiritual experiences, God, and Christianity. When I read over these journal entries today, I am uncomfortable with them. Something about them seems not quite right. Perhaps I feel that they are a little too detached, a bit too oriented from an observer's perspective. Maybe I was too one-sided in my approach to religion, too thinking, too conceptual. Maybe I was not honoring our religious urge as one of our great instincts. I'm not sure. But over the years, I've found these ideas have been valuable to me. I see the seeds of my book *Sacred Selfishness* in them. They were nurtured by the monk from my dream, whom I let into my life as a companion, teacher, and mentor through active imagination. I can trace other lectures to these reflections, and even sense new ones evolving.

In time, journaling, as an ongoing practice, helped me realize that to be alive, our religion, our spirituality, and even Jungian psychology must be lived. Living gives us the opportunity to create and find meaning, and our spiritual quest is to become whole, fully alive, and fully human. God lives in our flesh-and-blood experiences.

In Part 2 of this book, "The 'Cracking Open' Story," I moved from thinking about religion in a formal way, which has its own importance, to considering my actual life experiences. I believe this story honors *religio*, which means "linking back" in its essence. This linking back is the working basis for living into a future that is a true expression of our life. In this vein, we discover that there is often a heavy price to pay for a fulfilling life. Part of that price is to confess our own weaknesses and confront our shadow. Finding the courage and tenacity within us to pay this price gives us access to the hidden source of power within us, the Self.

❀ ❀ ❀

Three important images evolved from this period of personal work and are still integral parts of my life today. The first one is Buddy, sitting across from me in that Shoney's restaurant. He returned to me later in a dream. He looked at me intently and asked, "What have you done with my life?" His image has lived with me daily for decades and is still present, but his question has evolved into, "What are you doing with my life?"

Every day, I live to answer him. I am conscious of my elderhood. At the very moment that the great force of life brings my time to a close, I want to be able to look in Buddy's eyes and say, "I have done all that I can with all of my heart with your/our life." And I want to say, "I love you. Thank you."

The second image from these earlier times that has meant so much to me is the monk. He has been and is my companion. I feel he will continue to be with me in this world and beyond. He brings me comfort and direction. He keeps me in touch with the spirituality of the flesh-and-blood part of myself. And while he honors the thinking side of myself, he keeps that aspect in the backseat as we travel.

The third image is that beautiful, flaming image of Melusina. But she is complicated. I want to leave her for later, and perhaps for another book.

In the beginning and in the end, *Cracking Open* is a window into my life's journey—past, present, and future. It is about "burning away" patterns of living that had been imposed on me by circumstances and other people. It documents my sometimes raw and painful journey through the individuation process, revealing, I hope, how we can become aware of the Self by reflecting on the life we have lived and the one we are engaged in. (The word *engaged* here is a key word because if we are not engaged, we do not have much to reflect on.) Only then, can we come to love the Self's blueprint for us, God's intention for our lives, more than we care for the goals of our ego. It is in actualizing the Self's pattern for our lives that our lives become a true expression of who we are, rather than dominated by the needs and insecurities of our personal wounds and histories or the expectations of other people.

Again, as I have said, I hope my choice to share this personal part of my journey has been as helpful for you as it has been for me. Living this way brings many challenges, and yet I have found it to be our greatest source of inner peace and joy.

Author's Bio

Bud Harris, Ph.D., originally became a businessman and successfully owned his own business before returning to school to become a psychotherapist. After earning his Ph.D. in psychology and practicing as a psychotherapist and psychologist, he experienced the call to further his growth and become a Jungian analyst. He then moved to Zürich, Switzerland where he trained for over five years and graduated from the C. G. Jung Institute. He is the author of ten books, lectures widely, and practices as a Jungian analyst in Asheville, North Carolina.

For additional information about his practice and his work, visit:
www.budharris.com.

CPSIA information can be obtained at www.ICGtesting.com
Printed in the USA
BVOW04s2157020615

402966BV00001B/16/P